A Year With
Kurt Schwitters
2021-2022

Anthony David Padgett

catalogue...

Copyright 2022

Anthony David Padgett

THE ROMANTIC ART AND POETRY OF KURT SCHWITTERS - Essay
By Artist Anthony David Padgett -
Part Of A Year With Kurt Schwitters 2021-2022

After a year of responding to Kurt Schwitters' work, and the many influences and directions in his life. Here is an attempt to make sense of the changes in direction he made in his poetry, painting, collage, installation, sound art, performance and life as art. All this in the context of his journey from famous Hanover artist and poet to resettled refugee in the Lake District, England - the spiritual home of British Romantic poetry and poets such as William Wordsworth.

Our point of departure is to look at his art to help us understand his poetry. You can find my response to Schwitters' work mainly in chronological order to relate to the dates of Schwitters' work. Although much of Schwitters work is out of copyright, due to photographic copyright many of the images of Schwitters' work can be found online. Key notions I use in looking at Schwitters' art are expression, form and content. The Romantics explored nature from a position of awe at its sublime majesty. His Romantic sublime was the connection of his art to nature, his energy of expression and his interest in the materials he used. His main direction was less a Romantic in content i.e. the subject matter of his art. His was not a direct depiction of the sublime. Yet in Norway and the Lake District he also painted mountains and other such traditional Romantic scenes.

ROMANTICISM AND EXPRESSIONISM

Dada was an artistic movement that was a combined elements in ways that broke with common sense artistic convention. It began in Switzerland in 1916 and had a resonance for artists in post-war Germany.

Schwitters aligned himself to Dada and Expressionism, however, Richard Huelsenbeck (Berlin Dadaist) called Schwitters the "Kaspar David Friederich of the Dadaist revolution". In "Wanderer above the Sea of Fog" 1818 Caspar David Friedrich has a lone figure facing away from us, looking out over mountain peaks. This is a classic image from German Romanticism.

He was also called an "Expressionist in Dadaist clothing"

Schwitters was with the Sturm group of Expressionists. He danced with enthusiasm, and illustrated the program for the " Sturm Ball" with Die Quirlsanze 1921.

Schwitters was also expressive in how he organised collages and his impressionist brushwork incorporated feeling into his art.

In "Kurt Schwitter's Merzbau, the Cathedral of Erotic Misery" Elizabeth Burns Gamard says how both the Romantics and the Expressionists sought "Weltgefuhl" (world feeling), a mystical and poetic state of mind. This feeling equates to the Sublime of the Lake District poets.

CUBISM AND FUTURISM

Dada was noticeably derivative of Cubism and Futurism. The Dada with a purely aesthetic/formal use of materials was Cubist. And the Dada that had a subject matter/content was closer to Futurism - although Futurism was nationalistic and warlike whilst Dada was internationalist and pacifist.

Schwitters' work was largely formal and his innovation was to use rubbish, random and discarded items to create a vast body of works. He termed this with the random word "Merz". Schwitters' almost scientific investigation of materials had a quasi-metaphysical link to the sublime. And his work is similar to earlier celebrations of technology, e.g. Balla, Giacomo "Mercury Passing the Sun as Seen Through a Telescope" 1914 is similar to Schwitters' "Revolving" 1919

MERZ

Schwitters began to move on from Dada 1921 and stated he was against Dada in Merz magazine 1923. Part of the purpose of MERZ was to abandon reproduction, use materials not used before in art. Dada subject matter is nonsense, and Merz uses sense and nonsense as new materials. Dada shows oppositions and Merz reconciles them in a work of art. Merz is colour, line, form and material, painting is just colour, line and form.

As well as "found" elements (often print mistakes) having use in being a collage, the elements had a status in themselves as "Readymades". "i-drawing" was the basic unit of Merz - immediate and intuited, including elements as themselves rather than via an aesthetic composition.

His "Merz" period soon developed in 1923 with a Constuctivism period - where collage, scraps, objects are painted over. Merz was this ongoing relationship between Dada and Constructivism.

He continued to develop architecture, including rooms for mice, which changed as they moved around. His Merz stage (dada) 1918 collage and improvisation, shifting elements where the work is made in relation to the stage and not just the text. The developed into the stage becoming less central. His Merz-normal stage (constructivist) 1921 simple light, geometric - to facilitate the actors. Raised and inexpensive. Same props in all plays "Weltgefuhl" (world as cosmos and feeling of ecstasy). This interest in architecture and theatre laid the setting for his most innovative work, his Merzbau art installations.

And as well as art objects Schwitters also created environments, turning his Hanover home into a Merzbau. His Cathedral of Erotic Misery. This was started in 1923 as a Dada installation but as Schwitters became a Constructivist this style swallowed up his Dada reliquaries just as it also swallowed up Romantic grottos that were part of the work. His Dada work was overcome in struggle for pure form. And later it was to take on organic curves.

In Norway he saw the magic of objects and his organic work developed along with expressive painting, e.g. "Untitled (wood on wood)" 1946. It resembled some work by Dada artist Jean (Hans) Arp "Trousse d'un Da" 1920 and work by other artists such as Picasso, Henry Moore etc.

Schwitters' later work Untitled (Mother with Egg) 1945-7 was also similar to Giacometti, Alberto "Suspended Ball" 1930

REPRESENTATIONAL/FIGURATIVE

Whilst on this artistic journey he continued to make more traditional portraits and landscapes. He stated that his figurative work of nature is a source for pleasure and not needing to be art. And that he used painting to re-orientate himself. Throughout his career, even in Hanover, portraits were commissioned from him, flowers and landscapes sold he didn't attach artistic importance to them.

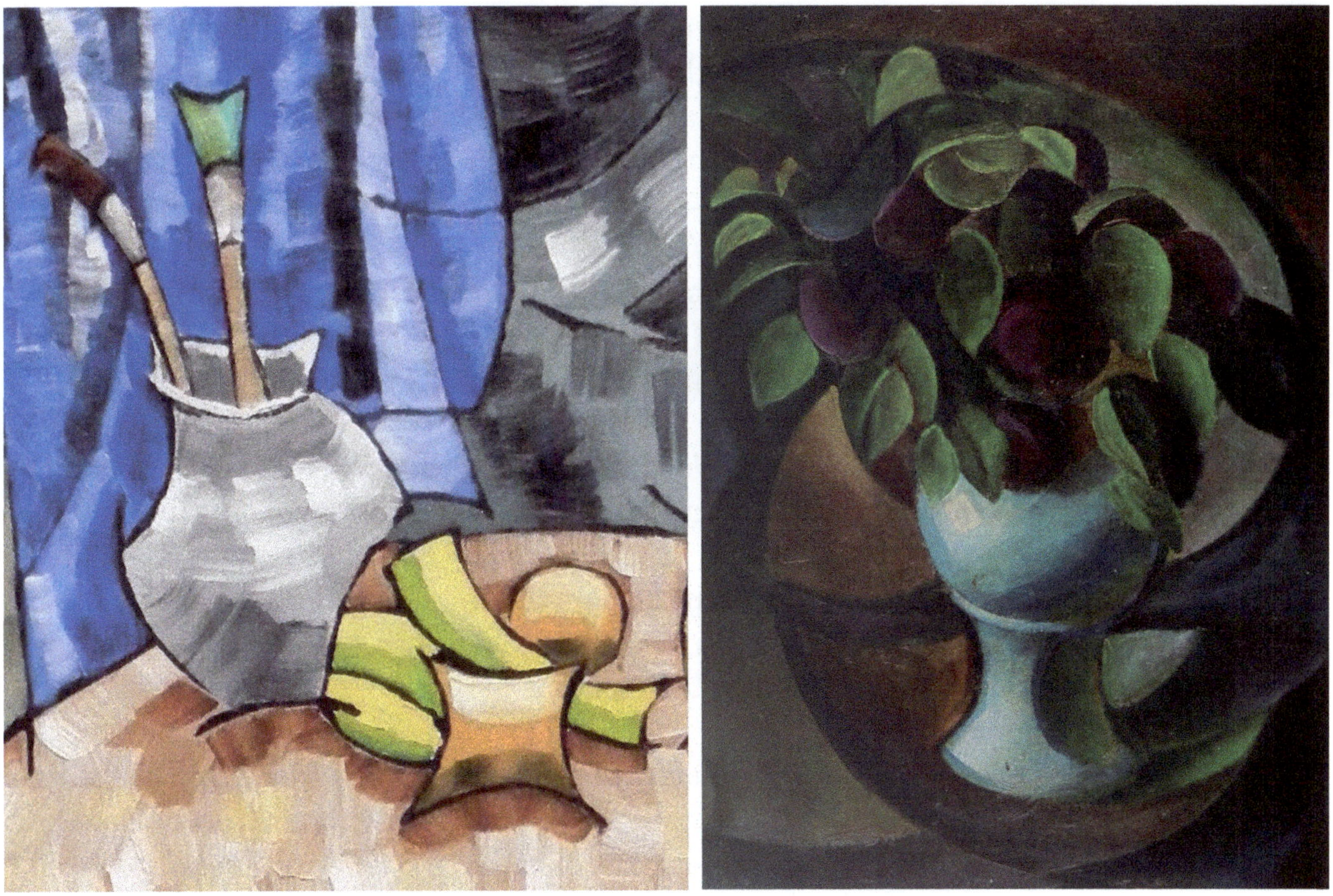

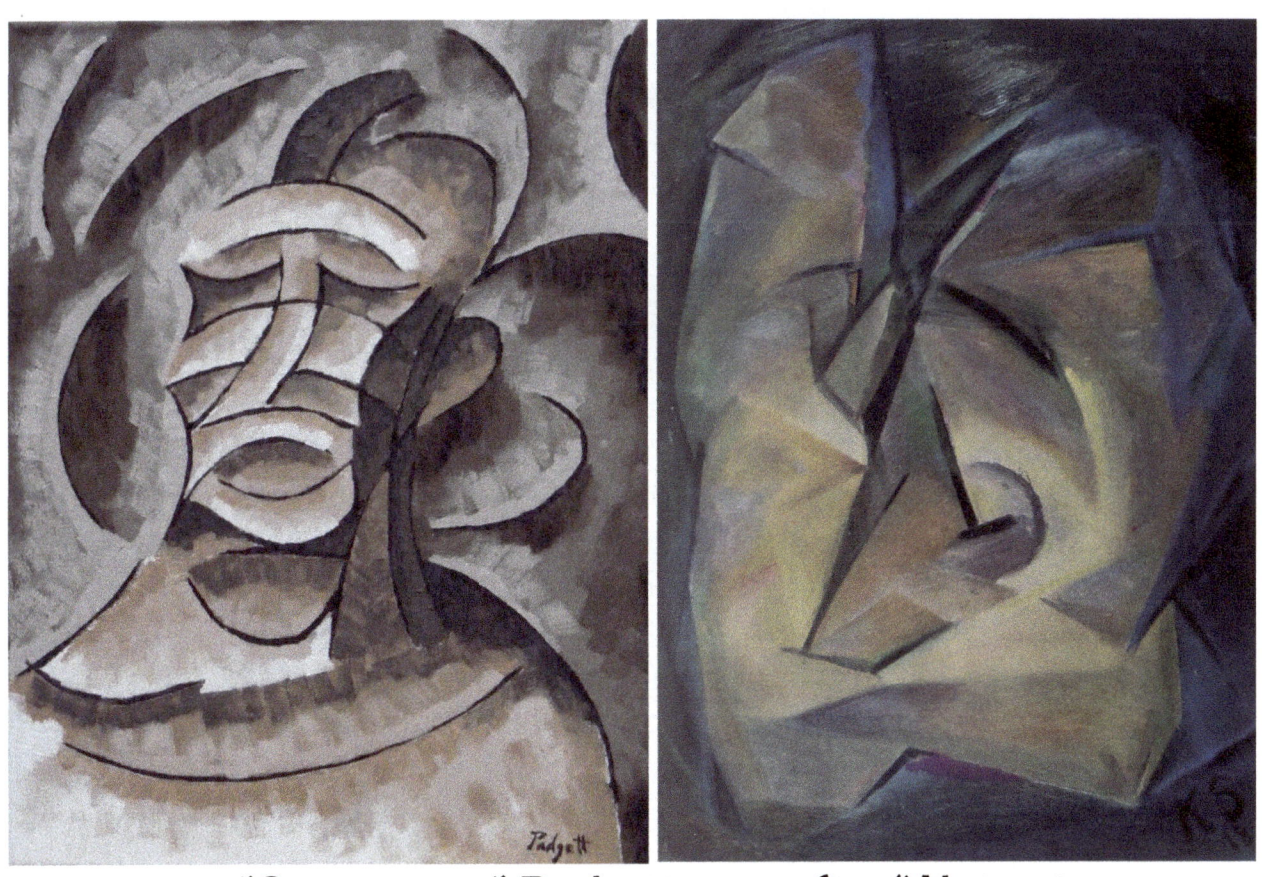

"Curvist flowers" Padgett 2017 after "Bou

"Curvist man" Padgett 2018 after "Abstract
No. 9 The Bow Tie" Schwitters 1918

Yet they were a key part of the development of his work. And in both his Merz constructivism and nature painting his relationship with nature was an important strand. "Whenever you are standing on a high mountain you feel free and happy"

His Merzbau in Hanover evolved from a Dada work into a Constructivist one. His second Merzbau in Norway was like that in Hanover, according to a Constructivist logic. And his incomplete Merzbau in England was more Organic.

The move was from clear, jutting outlines to amorphous, rounded shapes, from a Classical to a Romantic form. Was this a new kind of Romantic response to nature. A new sublime expression with echoes of the architectural style of Rudolph Steiner's Anthroposophy (linked to Theosophy).

By the 1930s the Romanticism of William Wordsworth was cliché and hackneyed. Friederich's "Wanderer" had moved from a direct link to the old Romantic sublime, to a domination and mastery of nature, as seen in Nazi Romanticism. In the late 1920s Lake District artist Julian Cooper captured a German Himalayan mountaineering expedition of Paul Bauer in 1929 before he joined the Nazi Party in 1933 and in 1934 became leader of the mountaineering and hiking division of Germany.

Schwitters reaction against National Socialism drove him to join the Social Democratic Party. This was mainly an expression of anti-fascism and didn't last. He rejected all forms of political art and didn't want his work to be used as a tool. His work was un-political but rejecting old power structures it is rooted in its time and full of political implications.

Schwitters' Romanticism occurred in his on-going journey of discovery and wonder in nature. His figurative representation of landscapes was nature on a macro level and abstract use of in materials was nature on a micro level.

This conjunction of organic Constructivism and expressive realism (in his paintings in Norway and the Lake District) led to some interesting cross-over artwork such as "Landscape of Grasmere" 1942 that did not seem to get fully resolved. And in addition to these developments he continued with his older styles of collage.

POETRY EXPRESSION

We turn now to the development of his poetry, which perhaps will throw light on his life and artwork. The perspective of Dada was to scoff, mock, ridicule and satirize, caricature with quotations and solecisms. This is not absurdity in pursuit of transcendent truth. It is a pragmatic a-logicality. Of artistic value and also a way to attack convention.

In 1919 Schwitters became famous for his poem "Anna Bluem". It was more expressive than Dada, and whilst Expressionist poetry was mocked by Dada Schwitters' recitation made it Dada. The main drive was artistic not political, social or ethical. He expressed the fragmentation of his age and the "desire to reclaim the rubble and debris of a destructive age."

Schwitters' poetry was also a form of collage and linguistic ready-mades. Collage is cut and paste whereas an I-poem is cut only, e.g. "pppppppp" 1923 which corresponded to a readymade i-drawing.

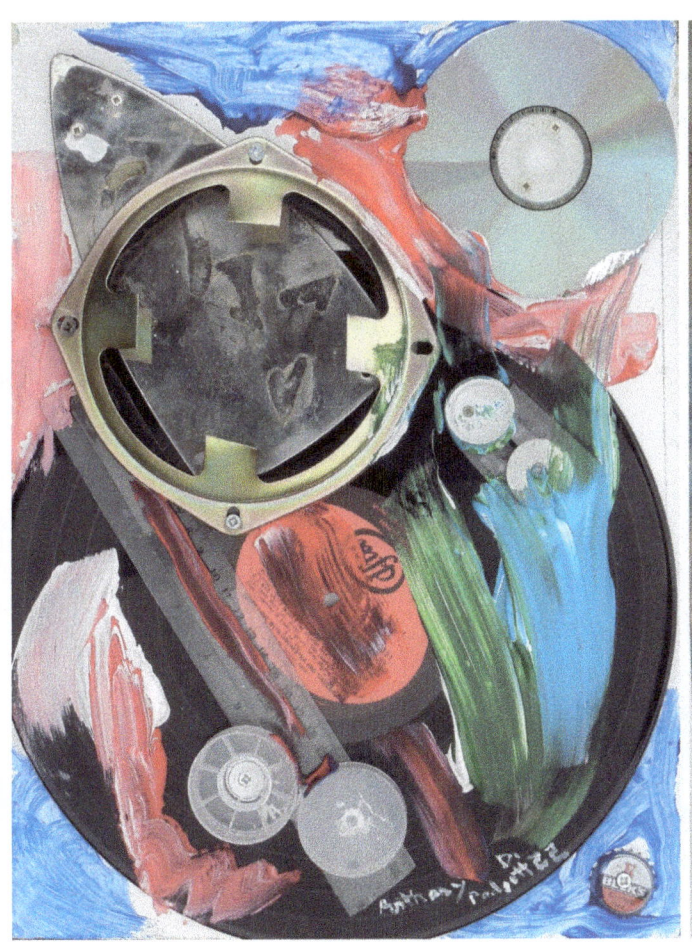
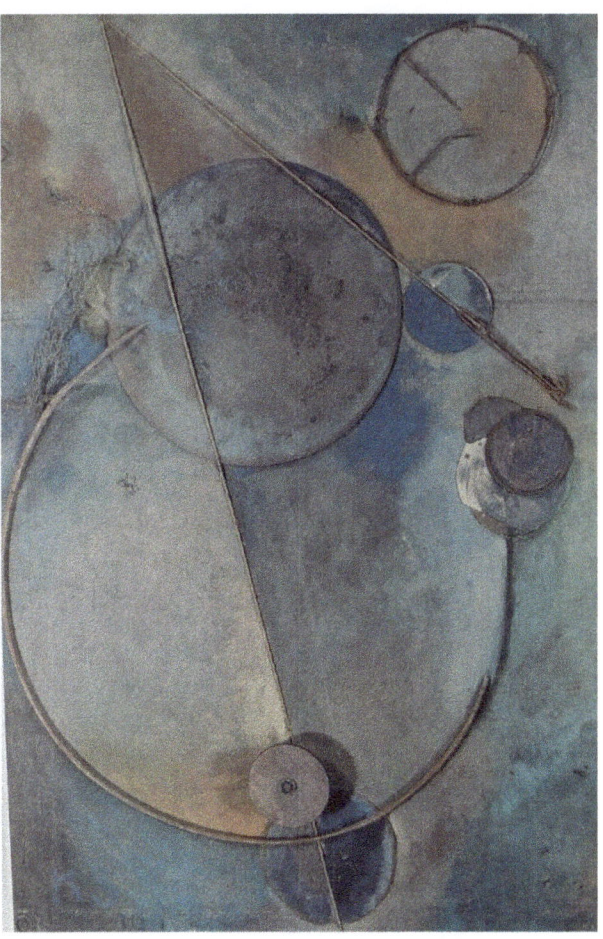

"Revolving" Padgett 2022 after "Revolving" Schwitters 1919

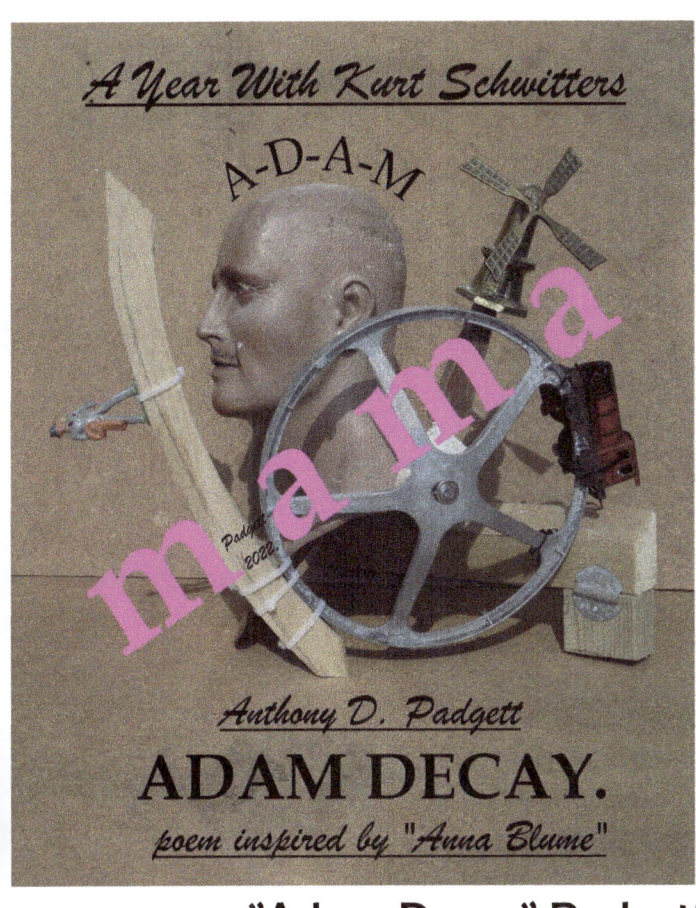
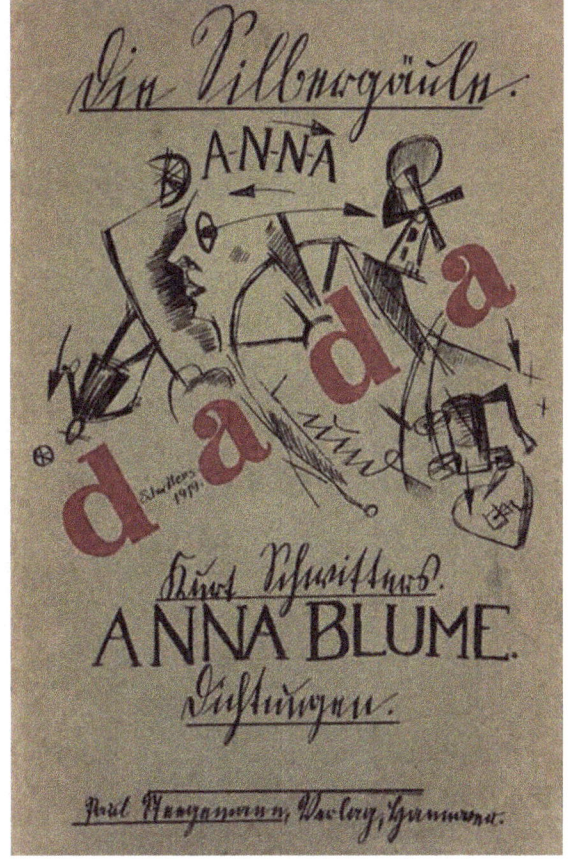

"Adam Decay" Padgett 2022 after "Anna Blume" Schwitters 1919

Adam Decay Off The Rails by Anthony D.Padgett 2022

We, spectres of intelligence,
We loathe ourselves!
We, you, me, us, our - them?
We are free, belonging nowhere.
Itemised, categorised,
Cognised - uncogniscious,
Anonymous and forgotten.
We care for the opinion of the ignorant
Our minds are our hearts and we feel with things.
With things we feel.
Goodbye green trees in open spaces.
Green we hate Adam Decay, Green we hate ourselves.
We, you, me, us, our - them?
We are free, burning dimly.
Green Decay, Green Adam Decay, itemising...
Ignored statements
X Adam has decayed off the rails
Y Adam is green
Z his rails still screech.
Loud is the taste of silent thoughts,
Soft is the screech of the buckled rails.
We complex beasts in our finery.
We hateful screaming rocks.
We loathe ourselves.
We, you, me, us, our - them?
We are free, fading fast.
Adam Decay,
Adam,
D-E-C-A-Y.
A flood of remorse,
An edifice of sheep.
We are ignorant, Adam,
We are ignorant of ignorance.
Inscrutable from all angles,
But we of ignominious ignominity,
We of and from all angles,
D-E-C-A-Y.
A flood of remorse,
An edifice of sheep.
We
Loathe
Ourselves.

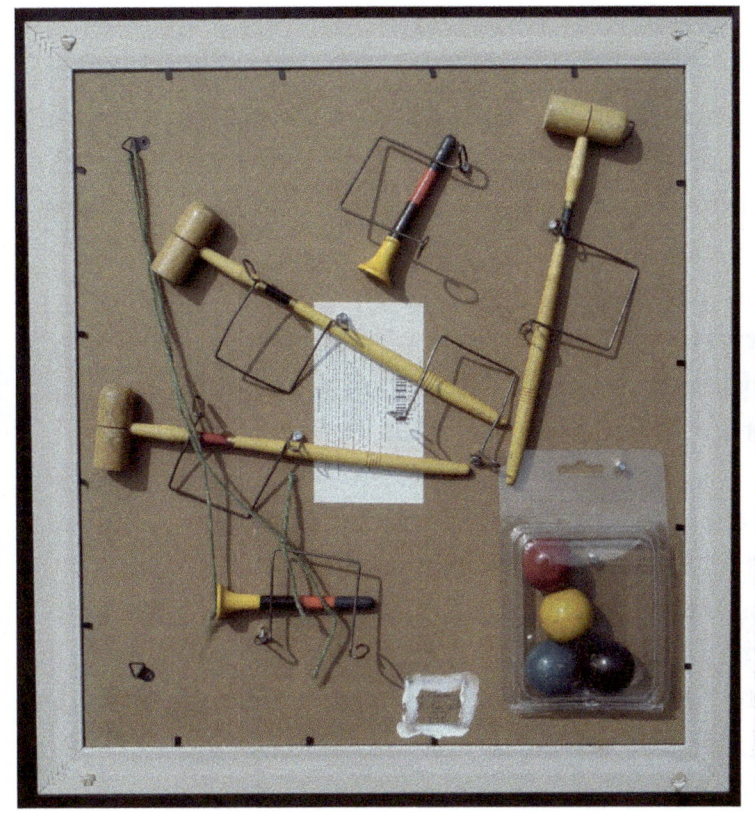
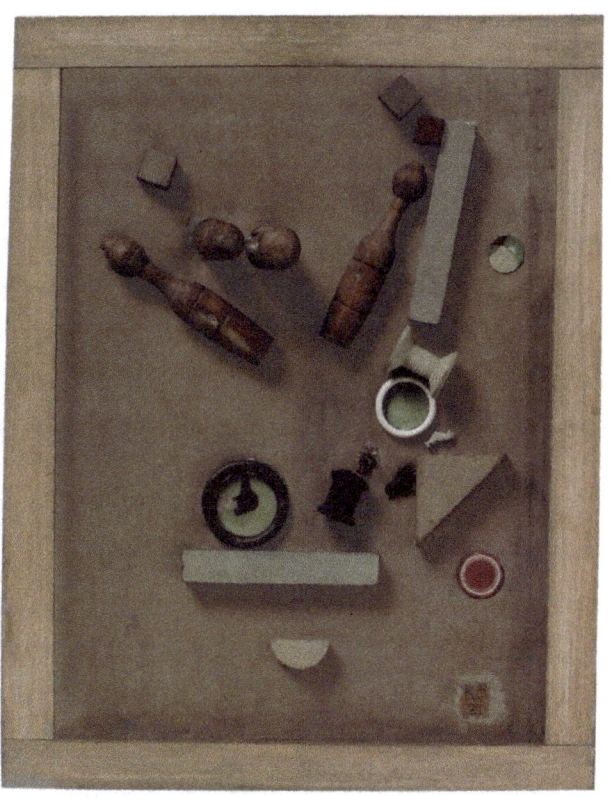

"The Croquet Picture" Padgett 2022 after
"Merz Picture 46 A. The Skittle Picture"
Schwitters 1921

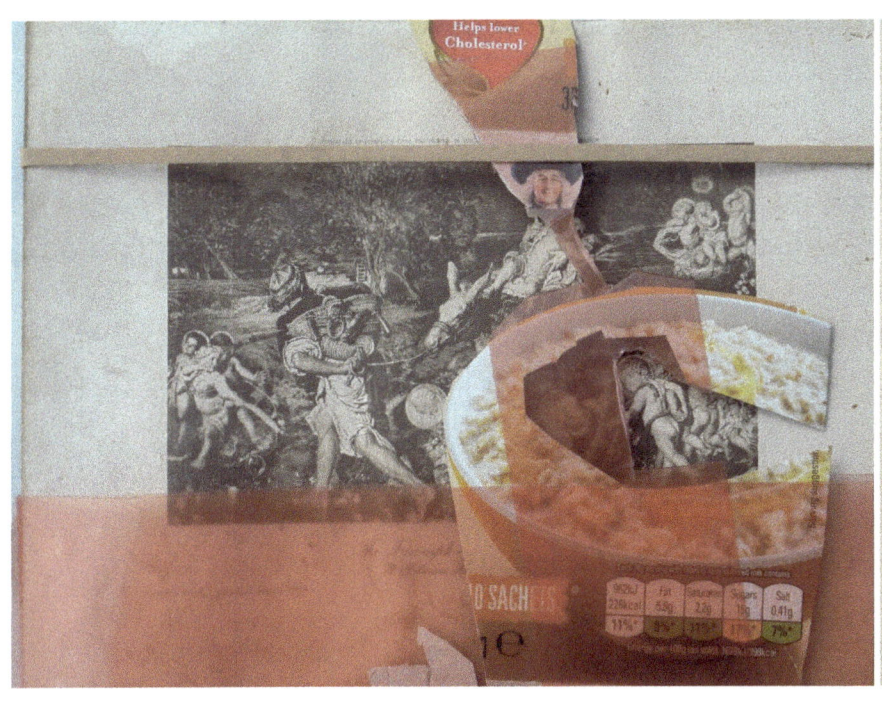
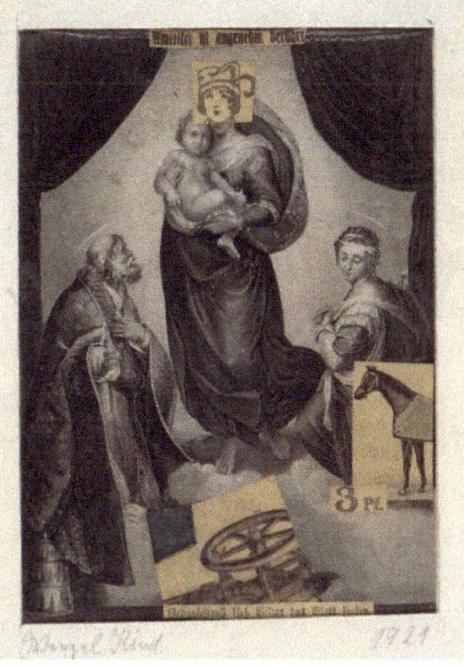

"Oats Knave" Padgett 2022 after "mz.151
wenzelkind" Schwitters 1921

Many of his poems were made with word association, no logical sequence or lyrical melody, no beginning or end, like a Merz painting. Letters, syllables, words and sentences interact and meaning is only one factor. Elements have their own sense. There is sense vs nonsense. Rhythmic sentences, fragmented sentences, words and fragments of words. Illogical and logical. Merz poems shed expressionism and included humour.

Parallel to this was his addition of Sound poetry. Was this a combination of both Constructivism or Primitivism, and the lengthy performance was an example of primitive insanity. This combination expressed in the Photogram of Schwitters in 1924 by the Constructivist El Lissitzky.

Werner Schmalenbach suggest that arbitrary language and ideas can generate "Weltgefuhl" reminding the reader of the world in its madness as cosmos and expressionist ecstasy. I think this seems more in line with the work and ideas of Anton Artaud and his Theatre of Cruelty of the 1930s that aimed to jar the senses to create a connection to spiritual reality. I wonder if Schwitters' connection to "Weltgefuhl" is more from his Romantic and Expressionist style than his Dada collage (poetic or artistic).

"Ursonate" published 1932 took 10 years to write and was both spoken poem and sung music. The word had sonorous value (i.e. as a sound) without reference to meaning, just like the Merzed collage. It was criticised by Dadaist Raoul Hausmann for being classical sonata. And Hausmann said he was given credit for originating the sound poems form - although Hans Richter said Schwitters gave the poem life as opposed to Hausmann's negative version.

The chronological order of Dada poets are Hugo Ball, Hausmann and then Schwitters. Ball recited his sound poems at the Dada "Cabaret Voltaire" founded by Tristan Tzara in Zurich in 1916. The cabaret had key elements resembling the Futurist Evenings (founded in 1910). And perhaps the most well know about Futurist sound poem was by Marinetti, Filippo Tommaso "Zang Tumb Tuum" 1914

And again, the Futurists prefigured this with their "Technical Manifesto of Futurist Literature" 1912 dedicated to liberating words from their Latin prison. Words-in-freedom. The first example "Battle Weight + Smell" 1912

August Stramm (killed in the war) influenced Schwitters. Also Hans Arp, the Dadaist poet. Also Sturm poet Rudolf Bluemner.

And prior to the way that he shaped poems on the page the Cubist poet Guillaume Apollinaire had created his Ideograms picture poems in 1914, and Futurist Corrado Govani's "The Sea" 1915 was a picture poem.

The physical cross-over of poetry and collage can be seen in his Merz magazine layouts in a combination of Constructivism and Expressionism. Again, different fonts and styles were preceded by "Lacerba" 1913-1915 the Futurist magazine that had a varied use of font and typesetting

Title page for "Dada 4/5" 1919 magazine by Francis Picabia was a Text cover like Schwitters' later Merz Magazines. Marinetti "Words in Freedom" 1919 is a Futurist example. And an earlier painted example is by Balla, Giacomo "Trelsi trelno" 1914. Other free word paintings include Soffici, Ardengo "BIF ZF + 18" 1915

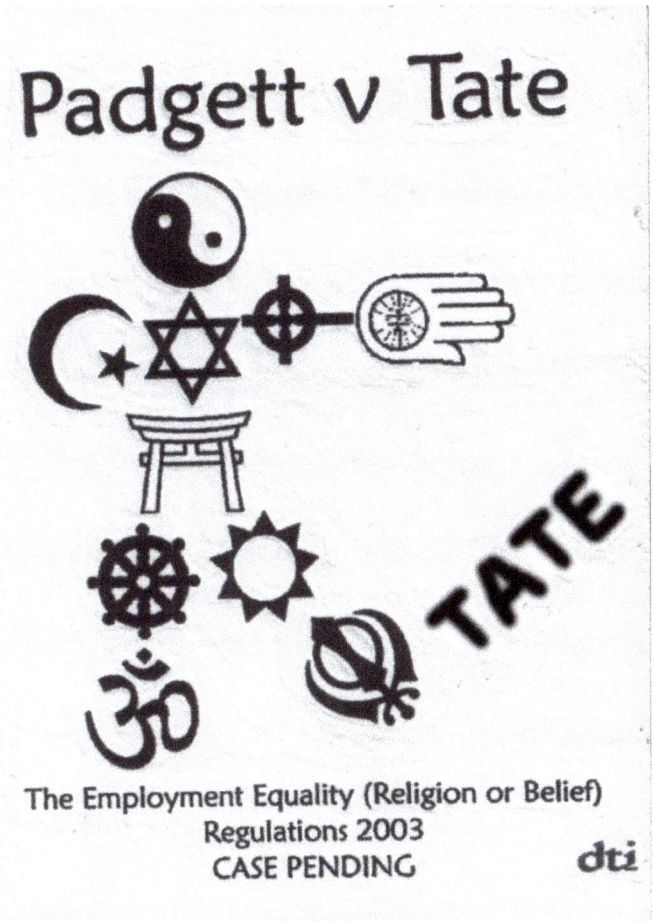

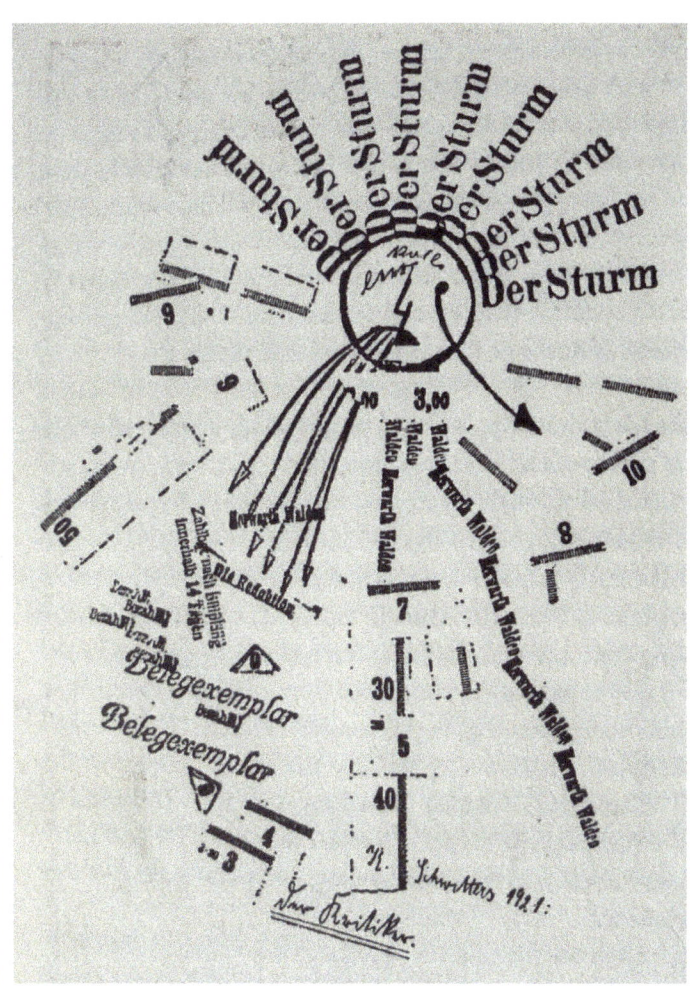

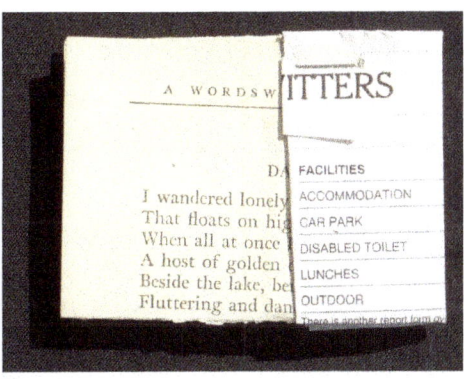

"Tate Case" Padgett 2022 after
"The Critic" Schwitters 1921

"Wordswitters"
Padgett 2022
after
"pppppppp"
Schwitters 1919

And in addition to these Avant-Garde developments Schwitters' poetry and prose also became more traditional in the 1940s, parallel to his more traditional painting.

In conclusion we can see how the development of Schwitters' poetry and art went through many already open gates, but he explored paths and expanded the range of possibilities for these forms.

Schwitters' life was fragmented, sense and non-sense, constructivism and expressionism, found situation and created identity. This mass of seeming contradictions is visible in his artworks. The Romantic's inability to comprehend in the face of overwhelming nature is mirrored in our inability to comprehend Schwitters' life. Ironically this allows us to give a sense of coherence to his life as a Romantic. Yet at the same time Schwitters employed many different styles and mediums without a need to unify them. We can oscillate between these two ways of seeing the man, united and divided, Romantic Expressionist or Dada Constructivist - which adds to the interest. His life was his work and his on-going journey expressed the chaos of life and the "Welftgefuhl" of his age. It is a journey it seems we have yet to complete, or perhaps we have no need to complete.

--- ---- -----

BIBLIOGRAPHY
1 - Tradition of Constructivism - Ed Bann, Stephen (Thames and Hudson) 1974
2 - Dada and Surrealism - Dawn Ades (Thames and Hudson) 1974
3 - Futurism - Tisdall, Caroline and Bozzolla, Angelo (Thames and Hudson) 1977
4 - "Kurt Schwitters" Galerie Gmurzynska 1978
5 - "Kurt Schwitters" Schmalenbach, Werner (Harry N. Abrams Inc.,) 1967
6 - "Kurt Schwitter's Merzbau, the Cathedral of Erotic Misery" Burns Gamard, Elizabeth (Princeton Architectural Press) 2000

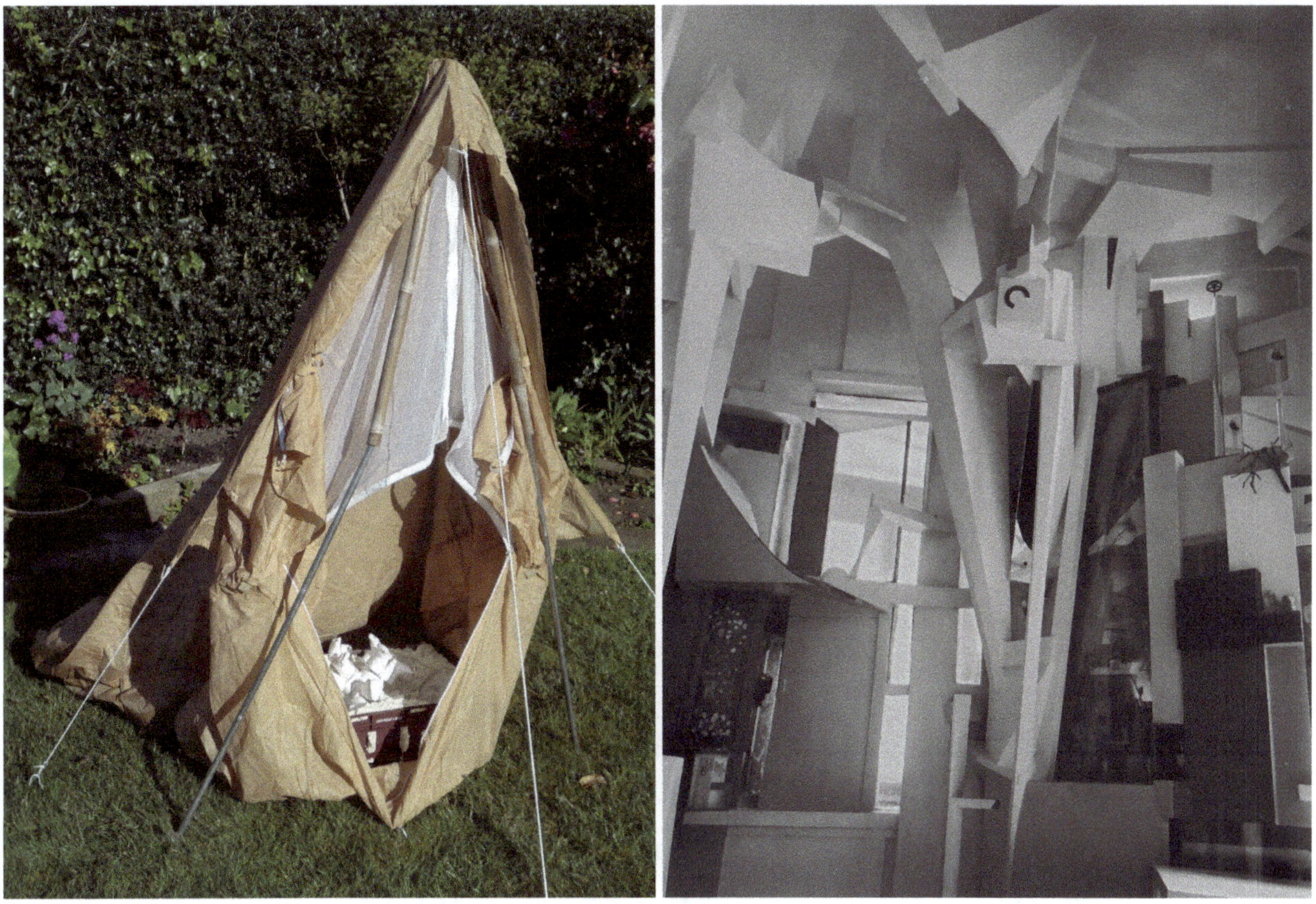

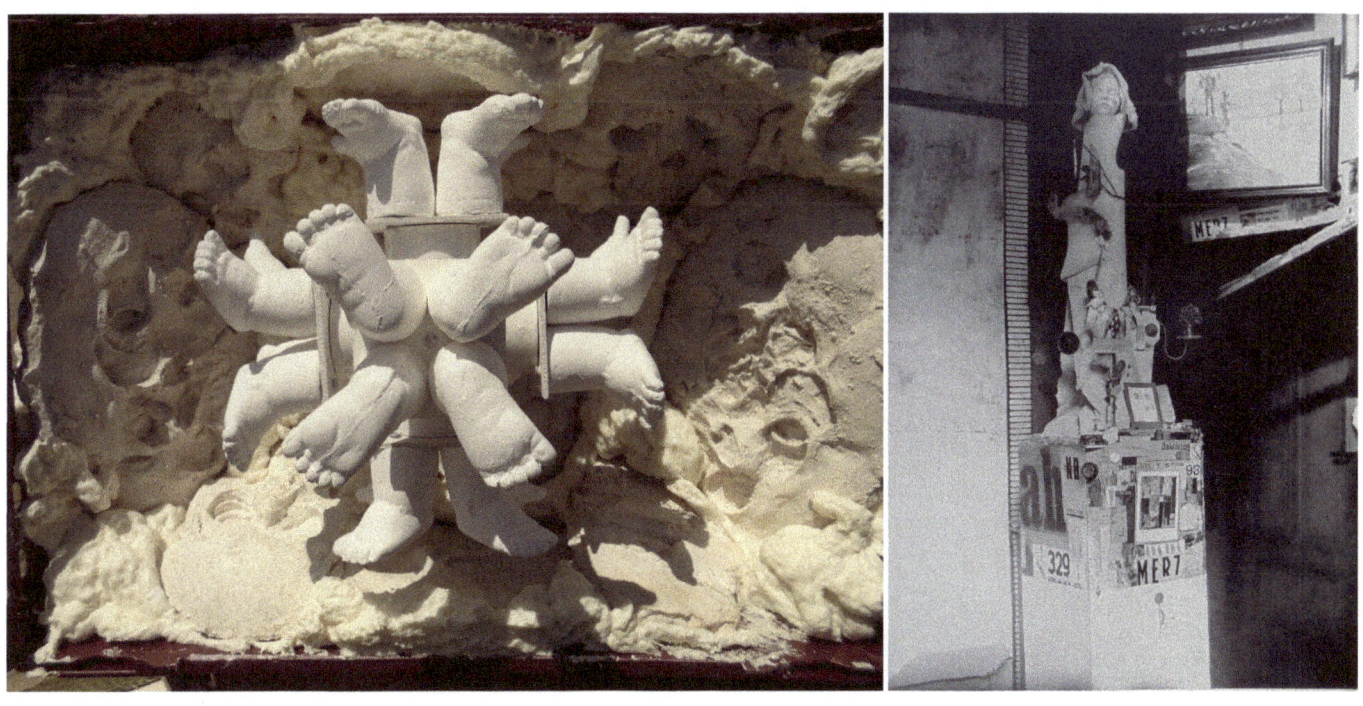

"Hovel of Thanatotic Joy" Padgett 2022 after
"Cathedral of Erotic Misery" Schwitters 1927-33

"Hovel of Thanatotic Joy" Padgett 2022 after
"Cathedral of Erotic Misery" Schwitters 1927-33

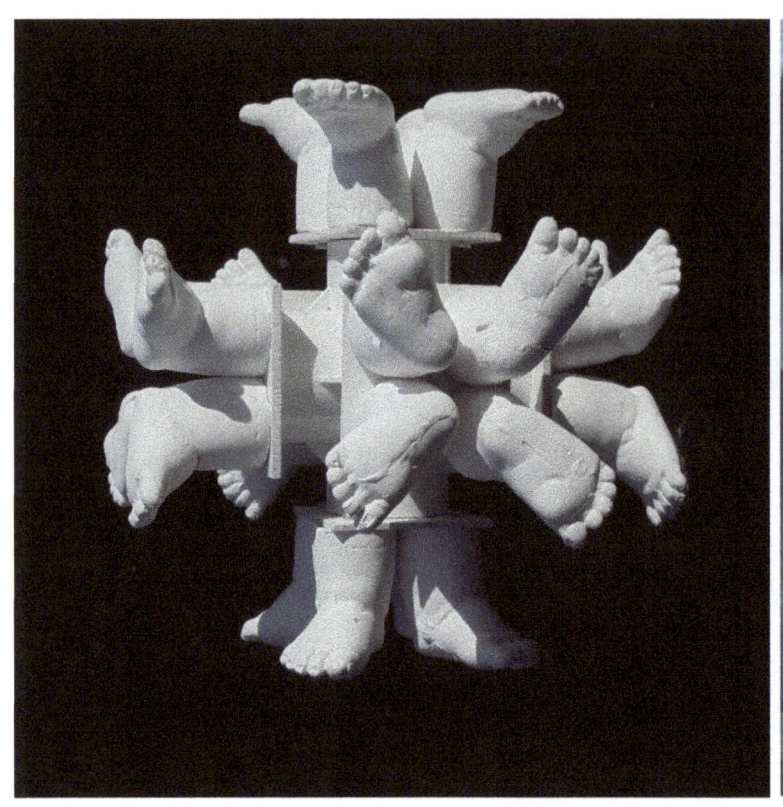 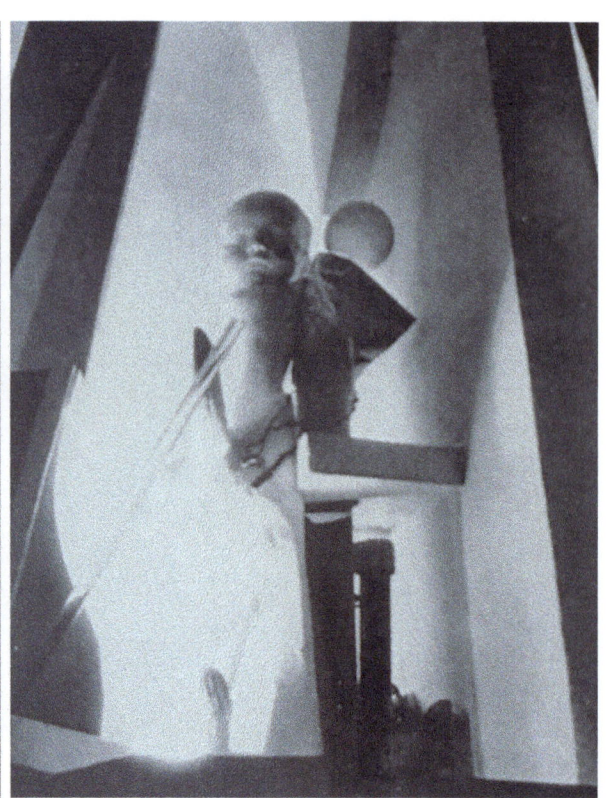

"Hovel of Thanatotic Joy" Padgett 2022 after
"Cathedral of Erotic Misery" Schwitters 1927-33

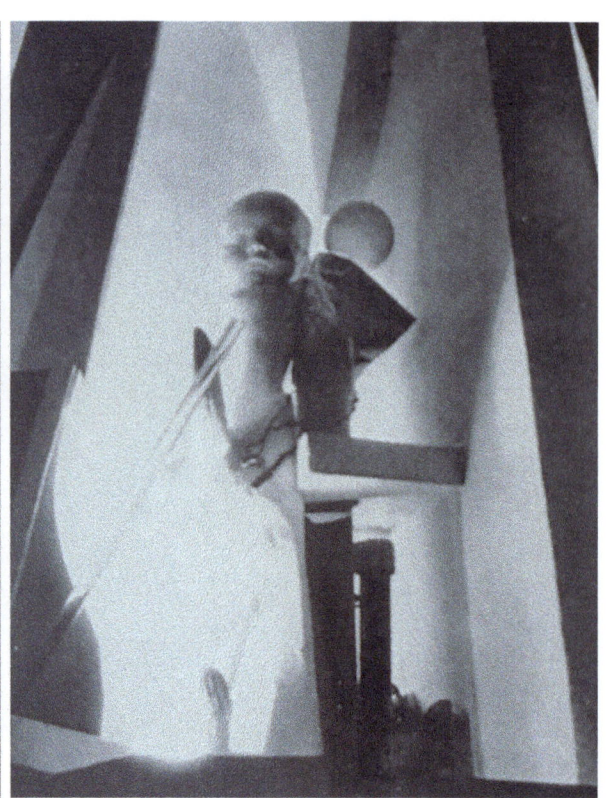

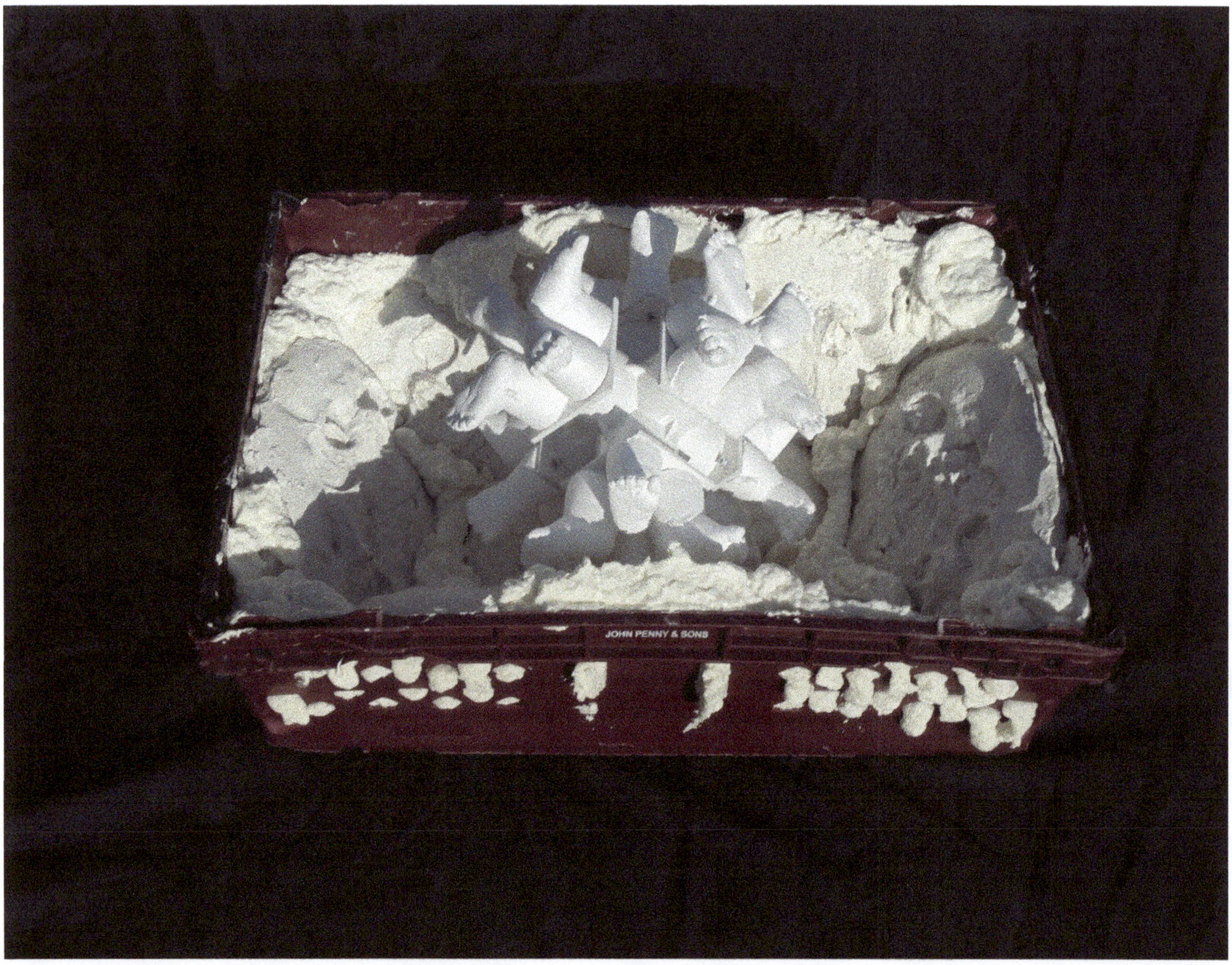

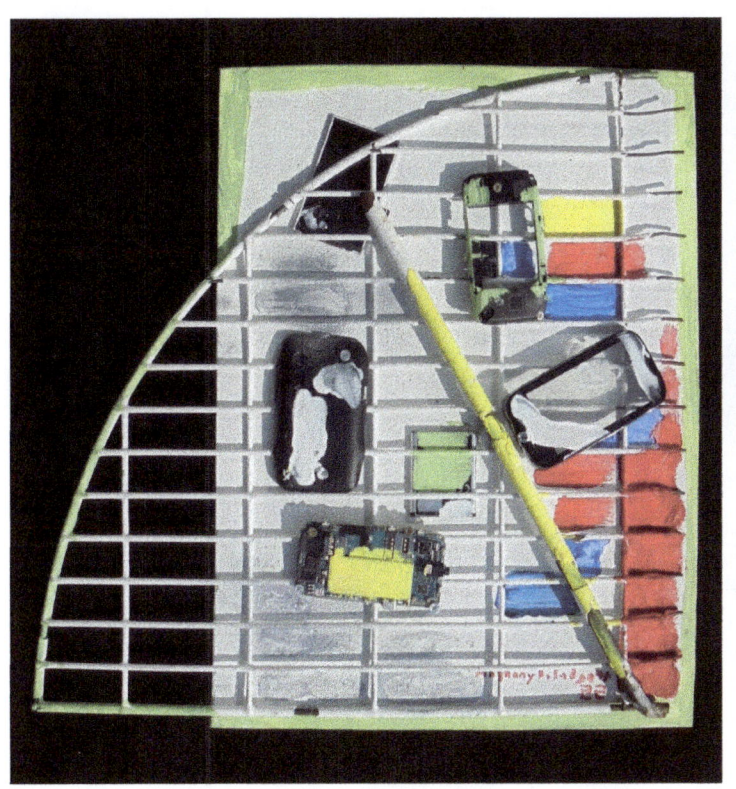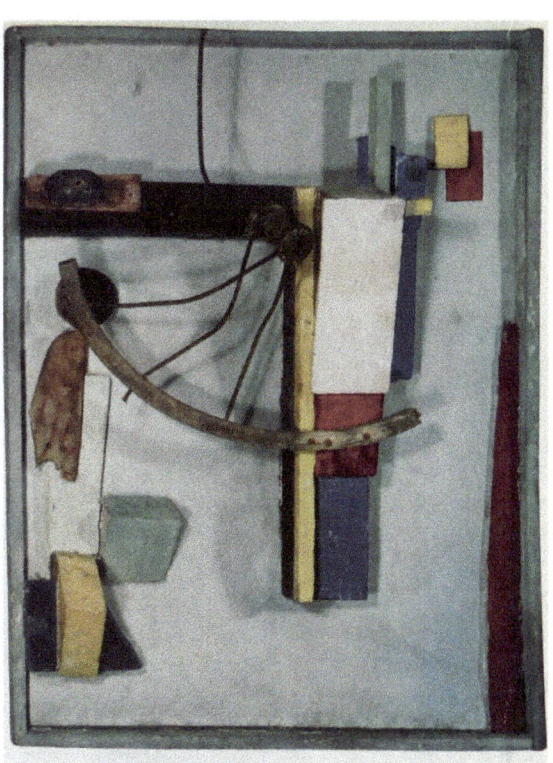

"Merz 1926 12. Little Sailors Home " Padgett
2022 after Schwitters 1926

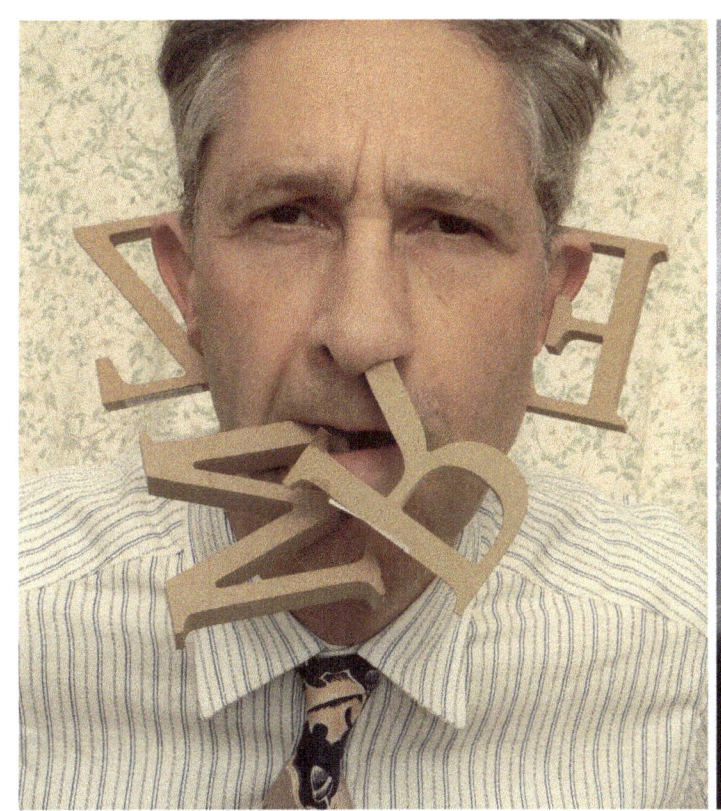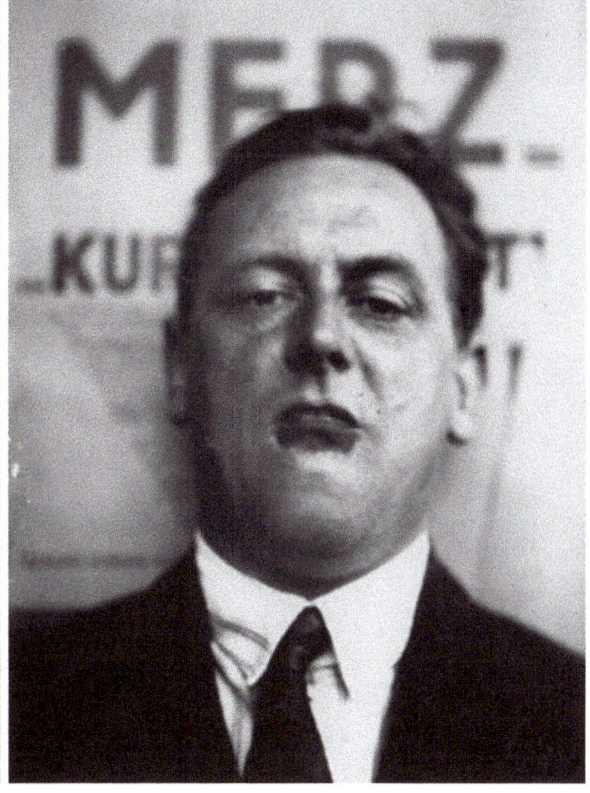

"Zerm" Padgett 2022 after "Photogram of
Kurt Schwitters" Lissitzky 1924

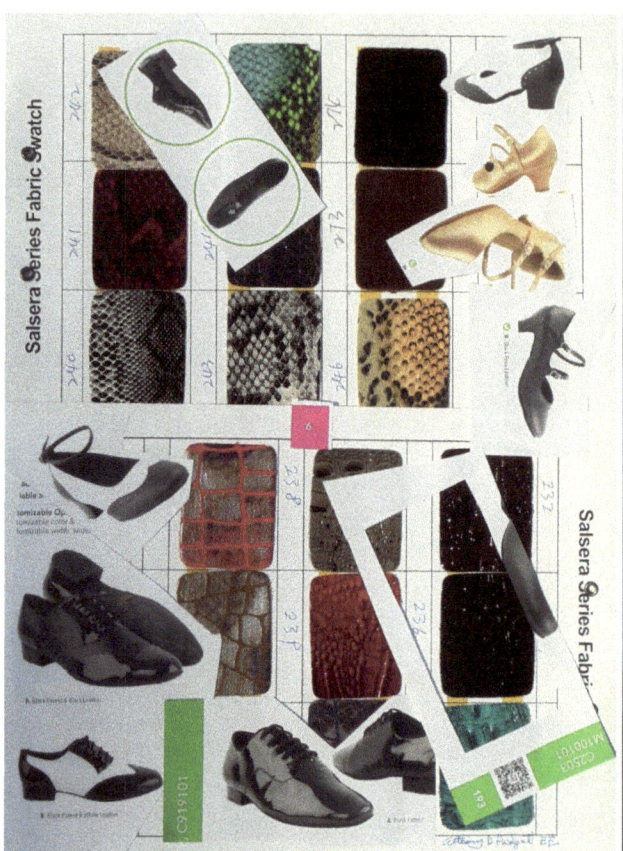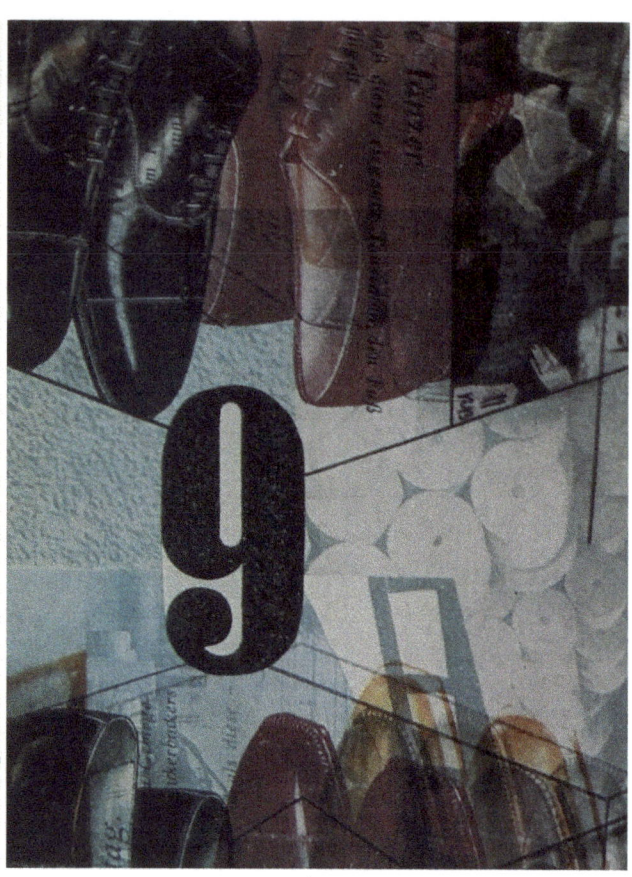

"6" Padgett 2022 after "9" Schwitters 1930

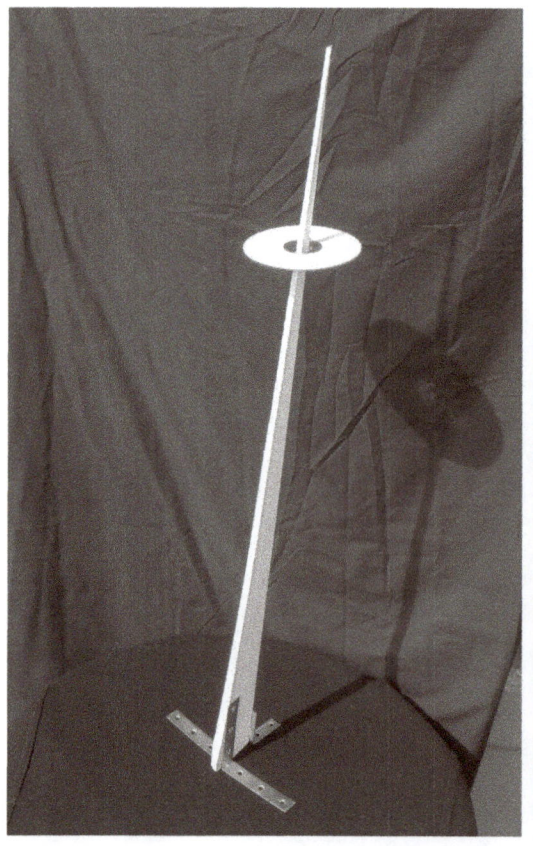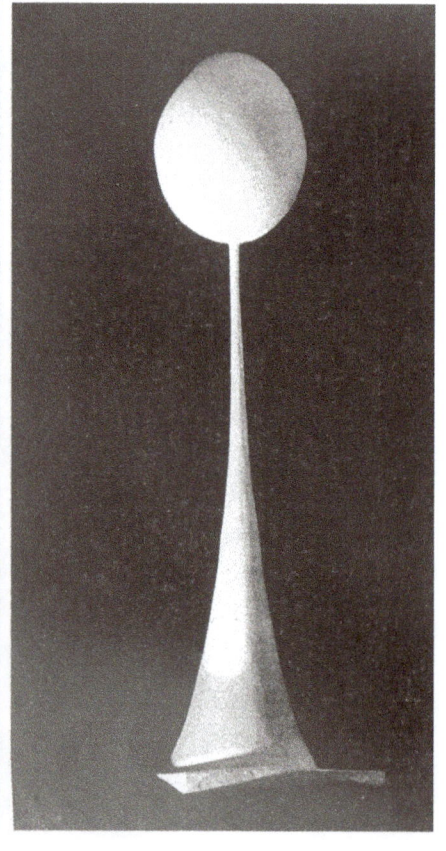

"Sculpture with Disc" Padgett 2022 after
"Sculpture with Sphere" Schwitters 1931-4

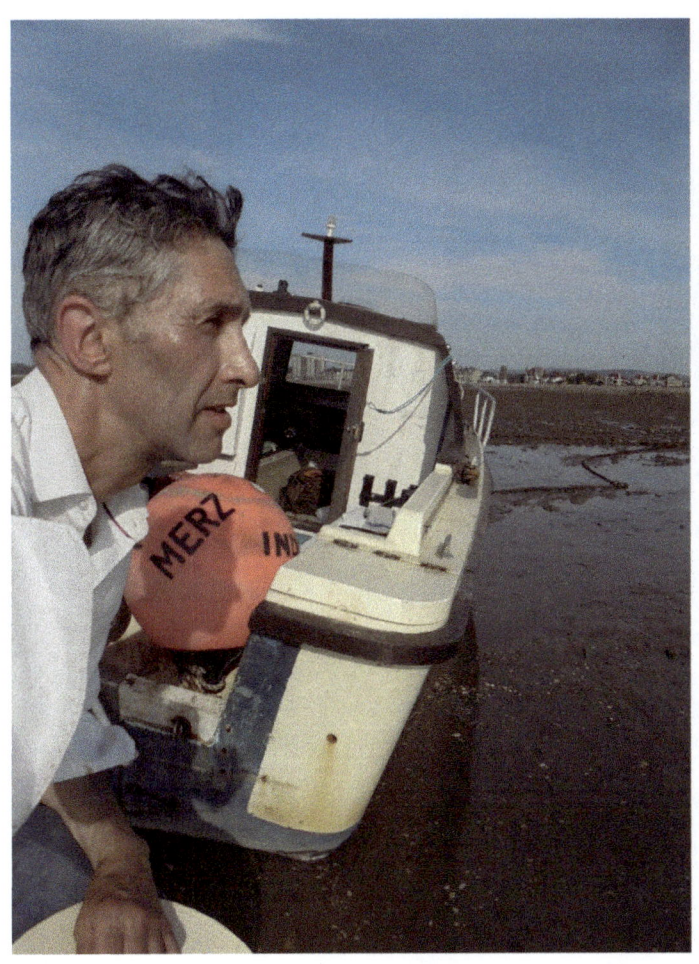
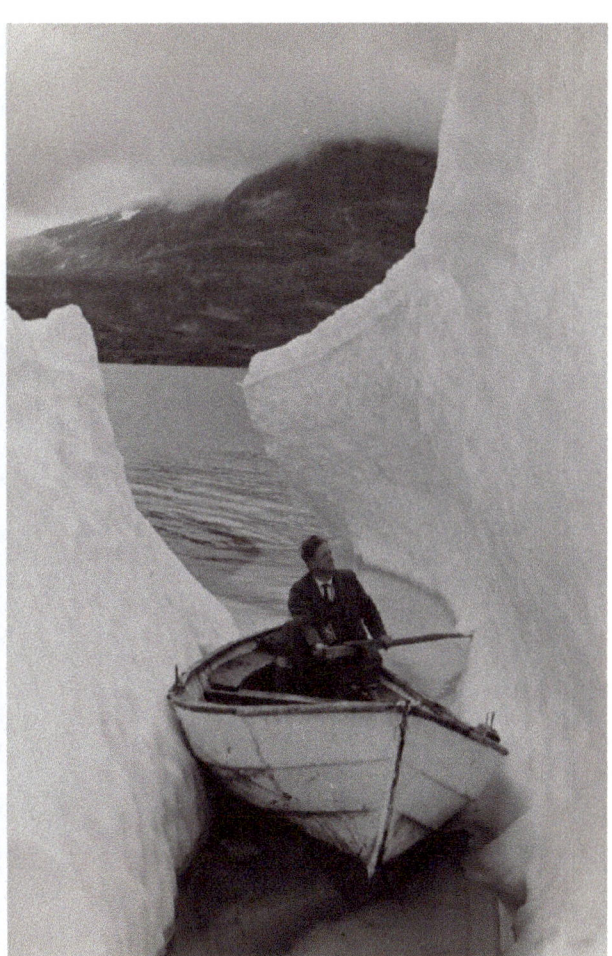

"Merz boat Morecambe" Padgett 2022 after
Schwitters in Norway by Ernst Schwitters 1937

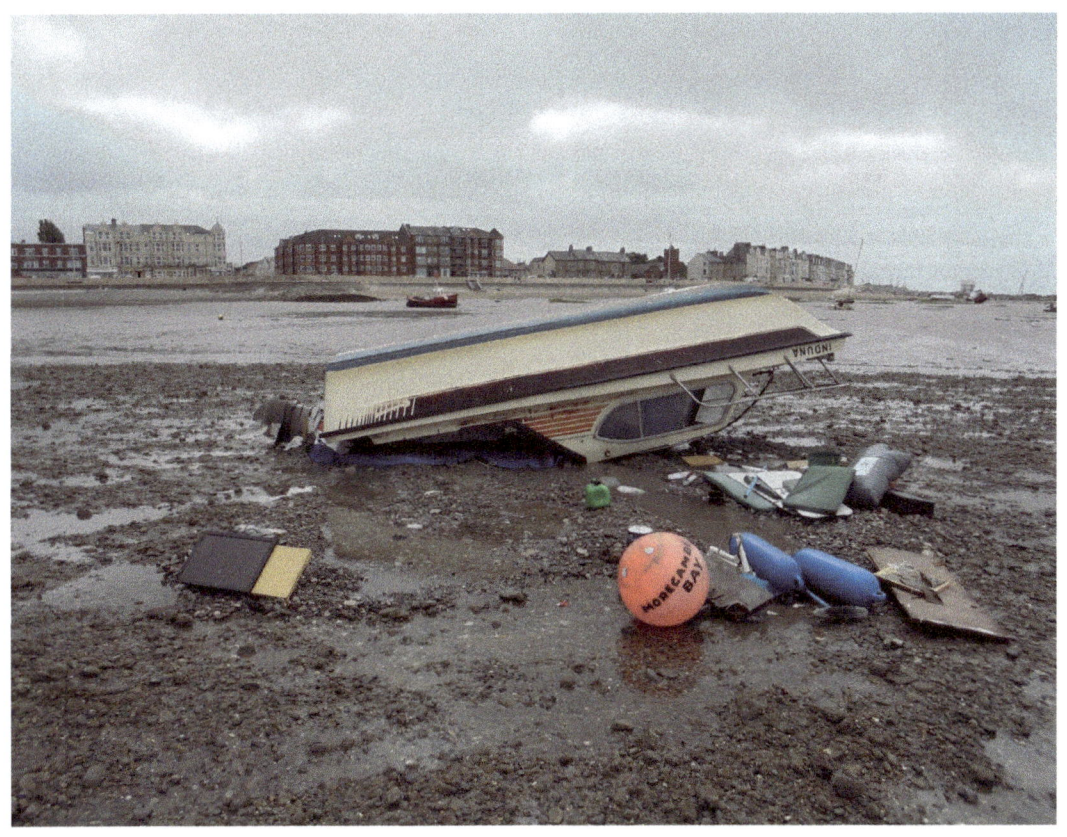

"Merz boat Morecambe" Padgett 2022 after
Schwitters in Norway by Ernst Schwitters 1937

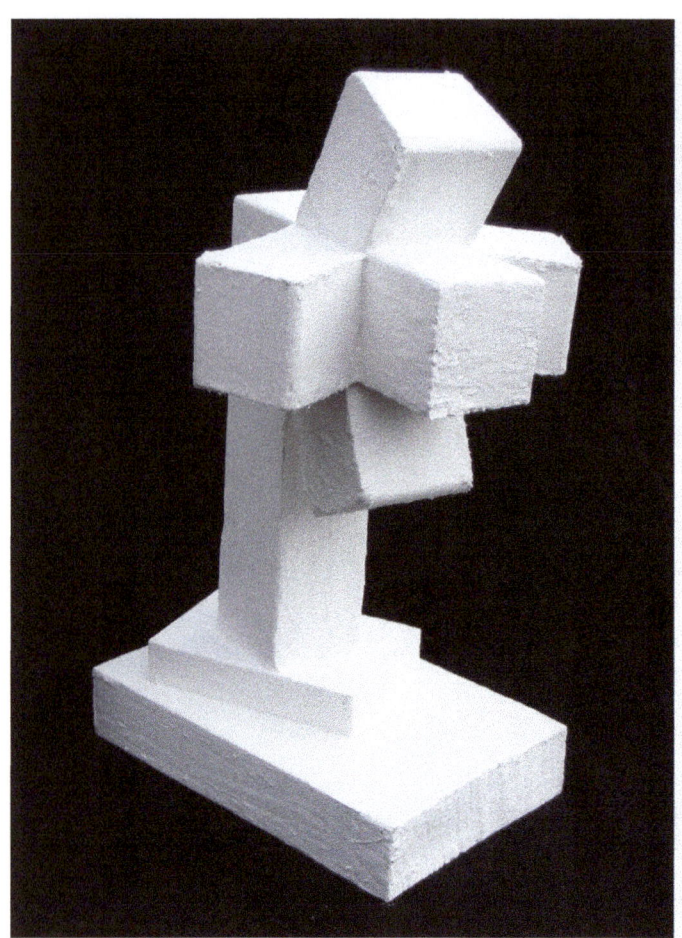
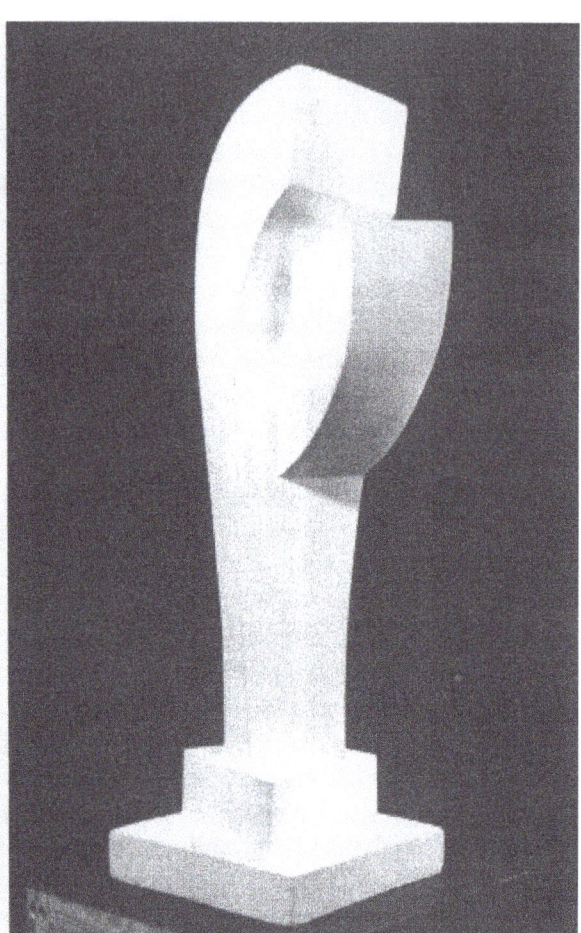

"Spring Daffodil" Padgett 2022 after
"Autumn Crocus" Schwitters 1926-8

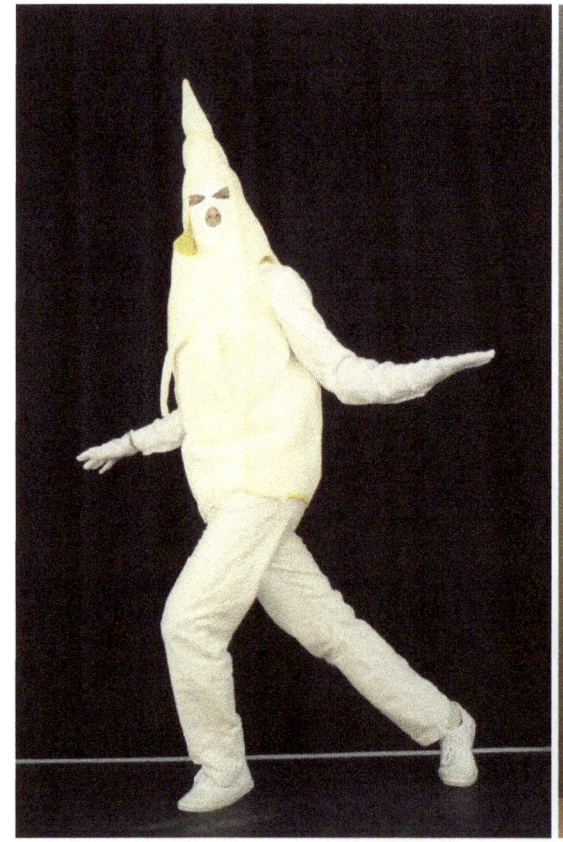
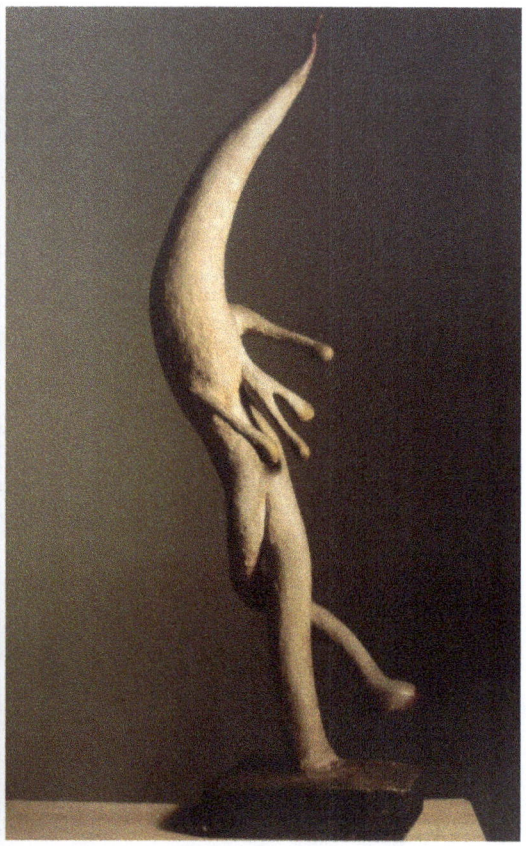

"Merz Dance" Padgett 2022 after "Dancer"
Schwitters 1943

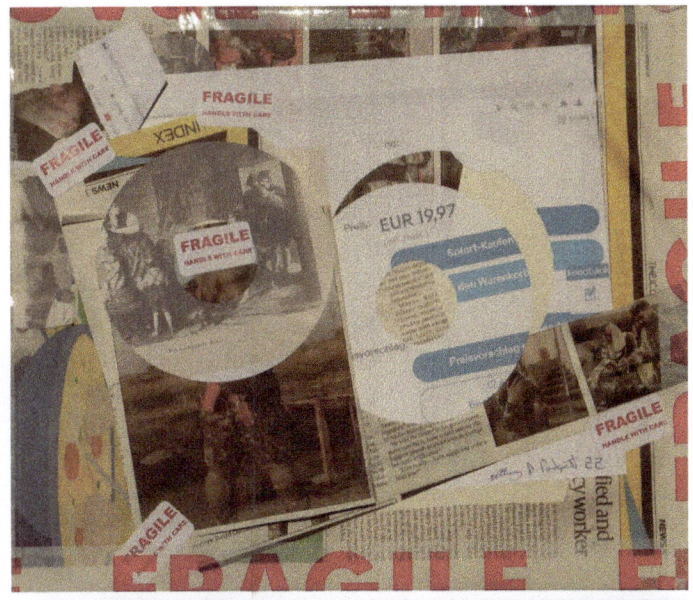

"Ukraine War" Padgett
2022 after "untitled the
wounded hunter"
Schwitters 1919

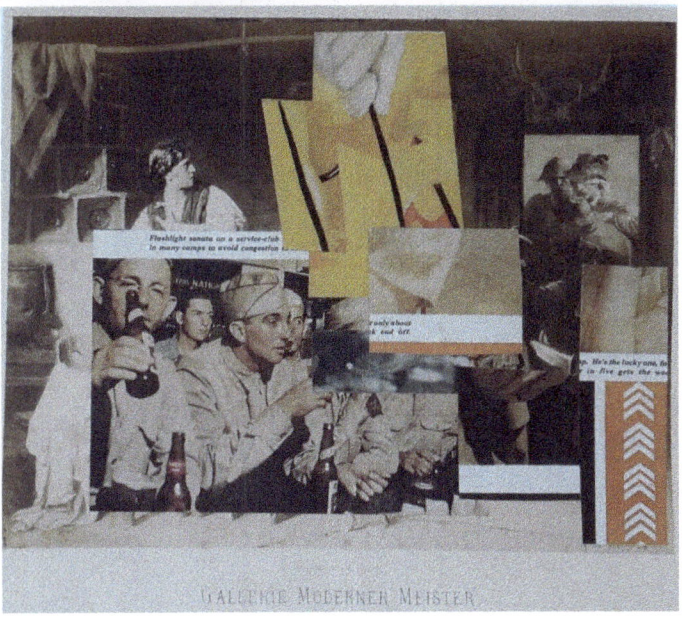

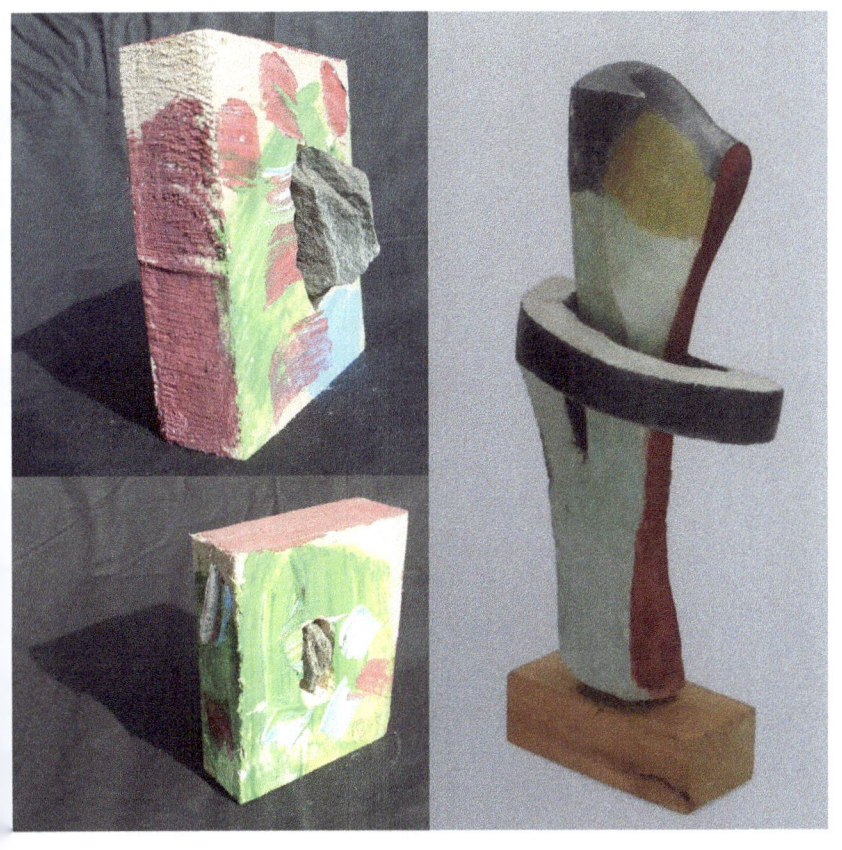

"Penetrating
Sculpture"
Padgett 2022
after "The All
Embracing Sculp-
ture" Schwitters
1942-5

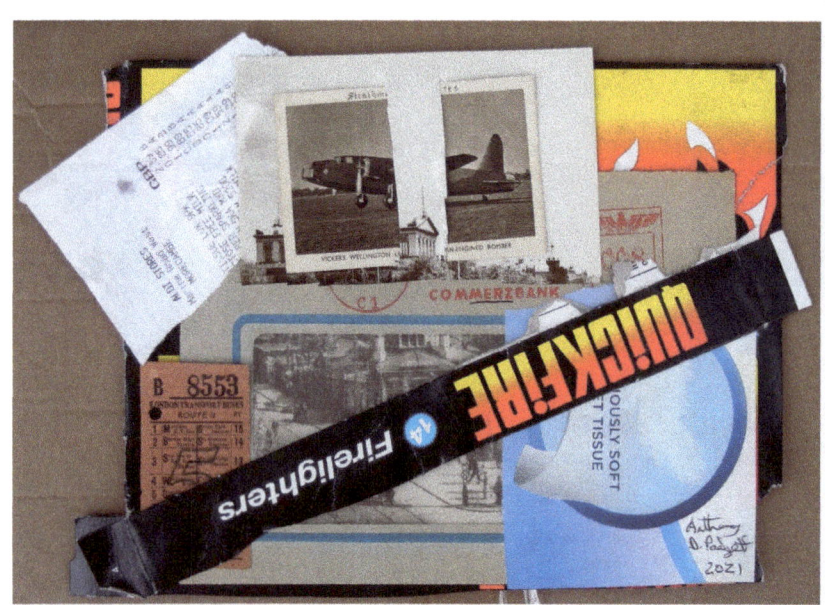
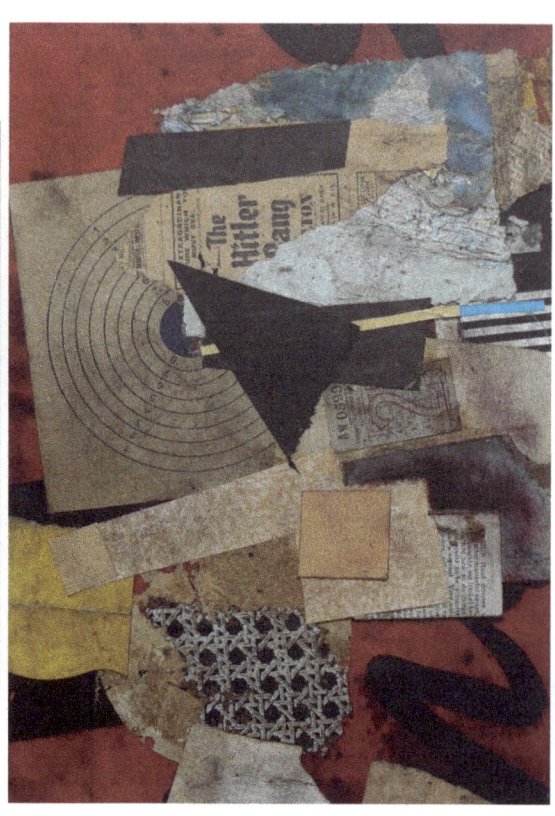

"The Churchill Gang" Padgett 20212 after "The Hitler Gang" Schwitters 1944

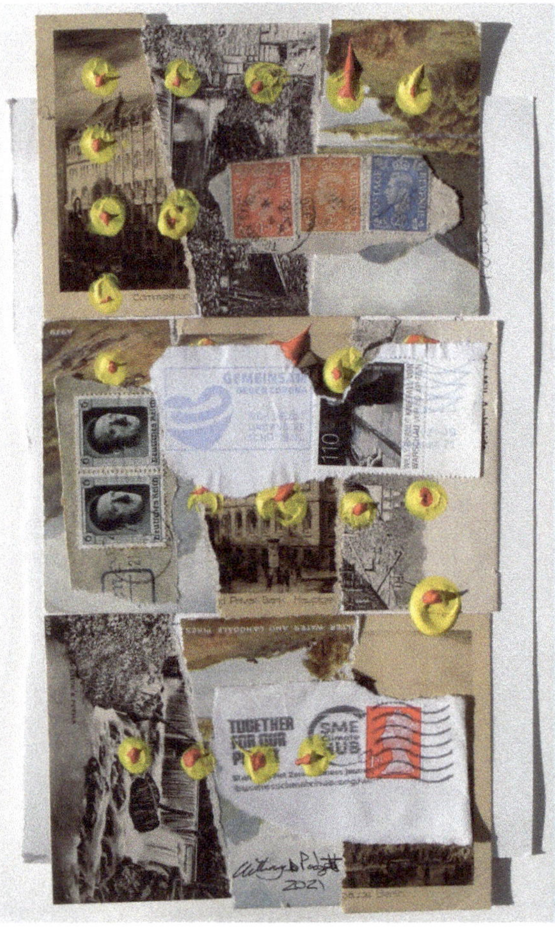

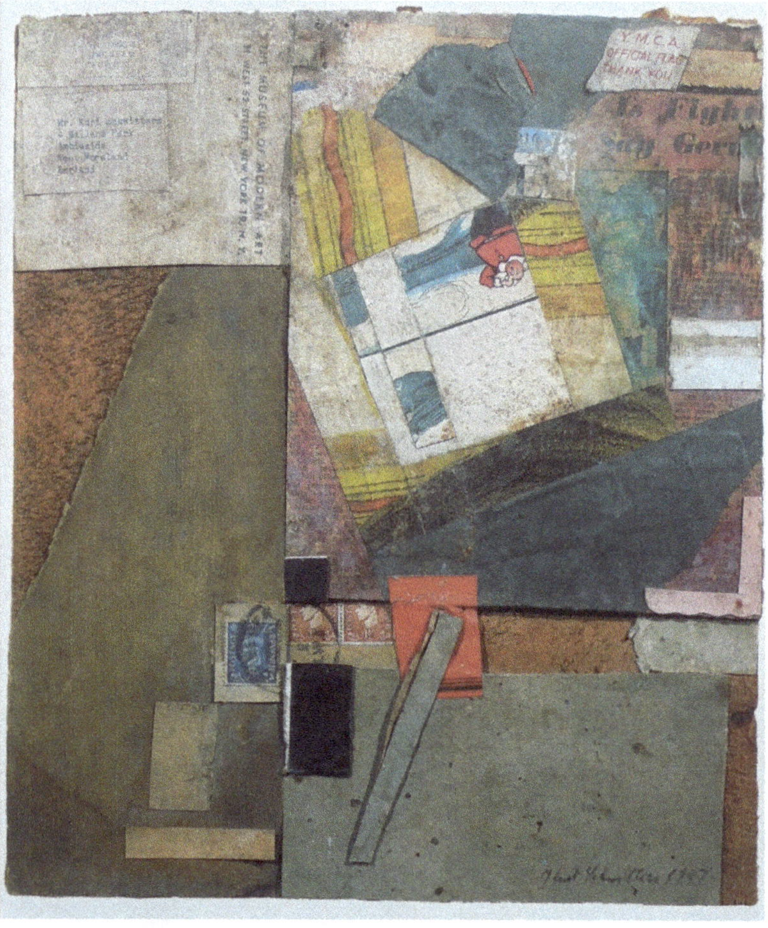

"Merzman" Padgett 2021 after "YMCA official flag thank you" Schwitters 1947

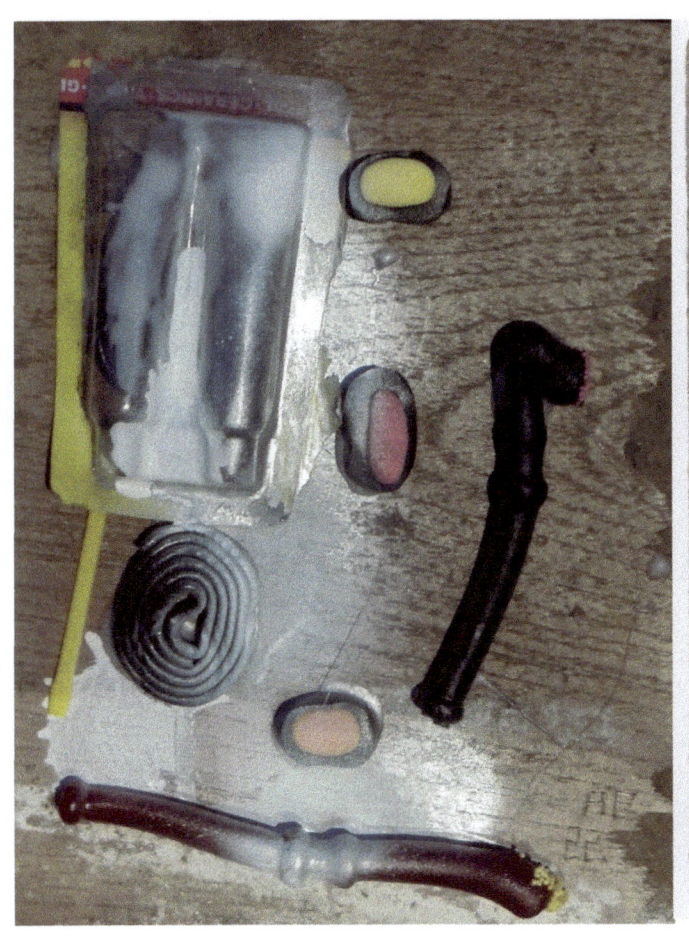

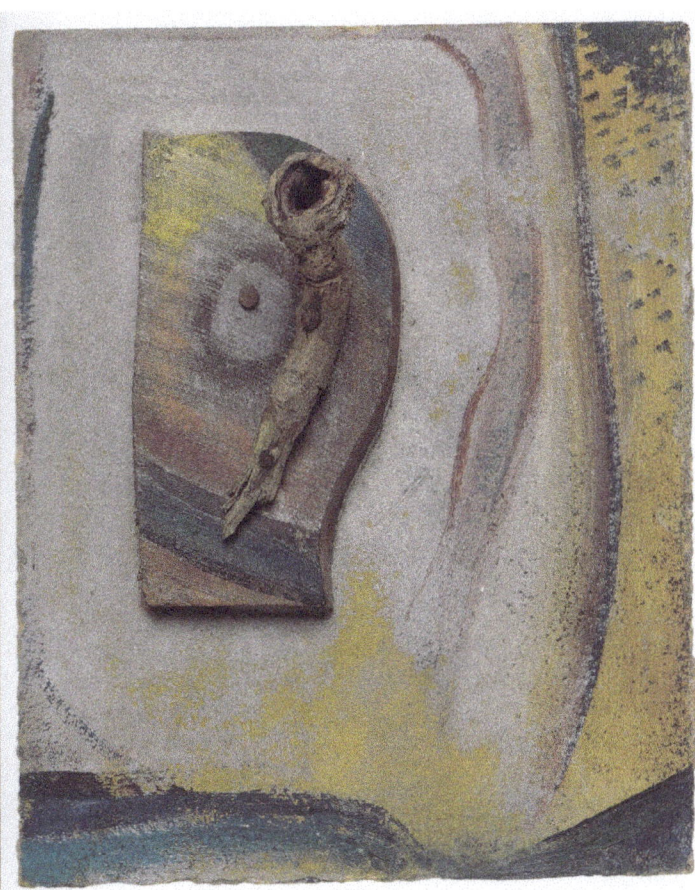

"Sweet Pipe" Padgett 2022
after "Untitled (wood on wood)"
Schwitters 1946

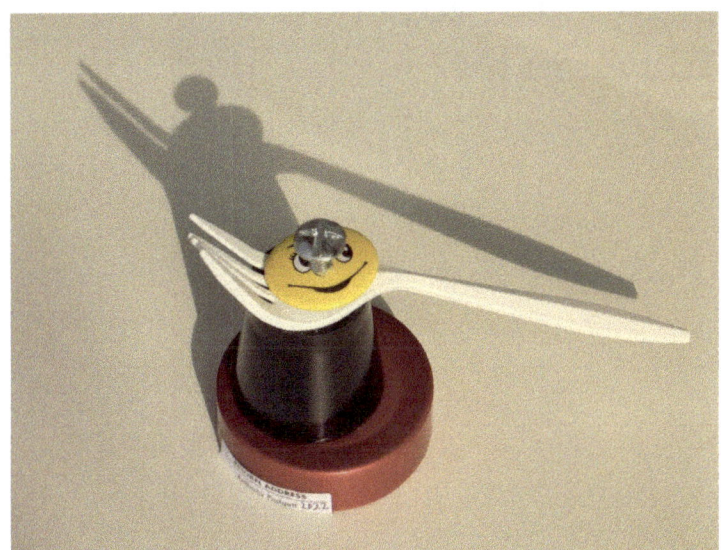

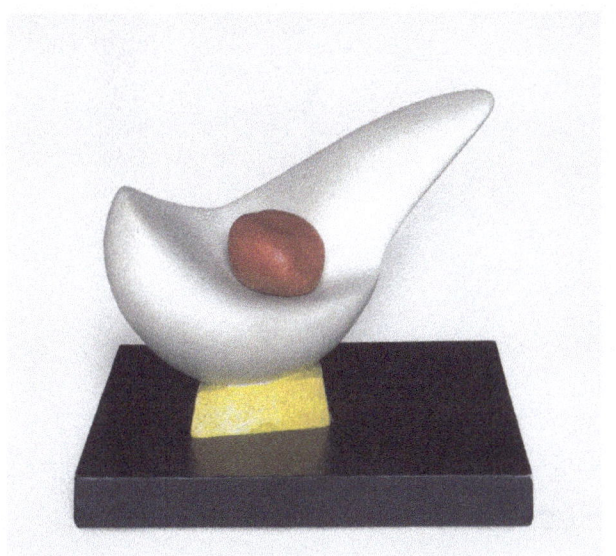

"Face Fork" Padgett 2022
after "untitled Mother and
Egg" Schwitters 1946

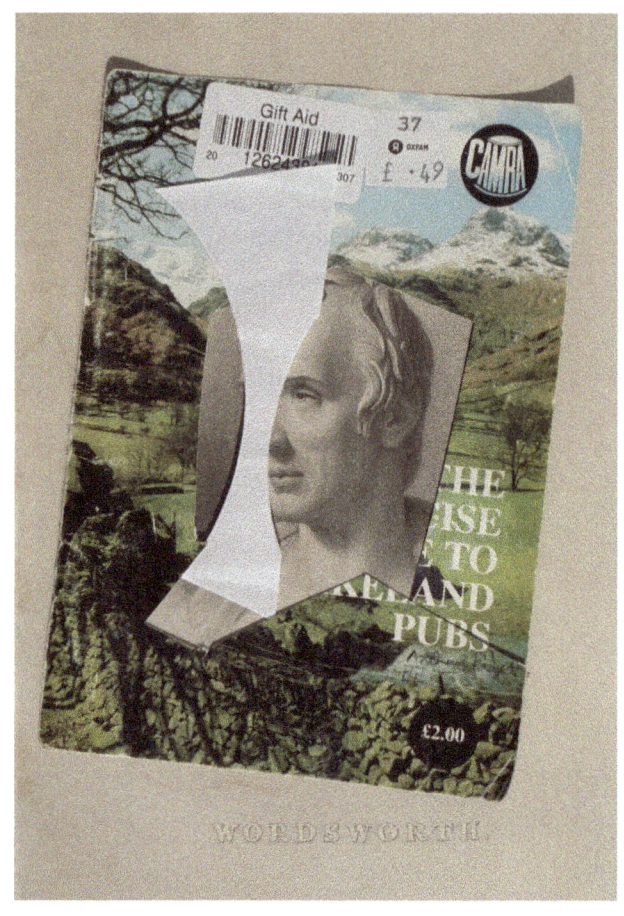

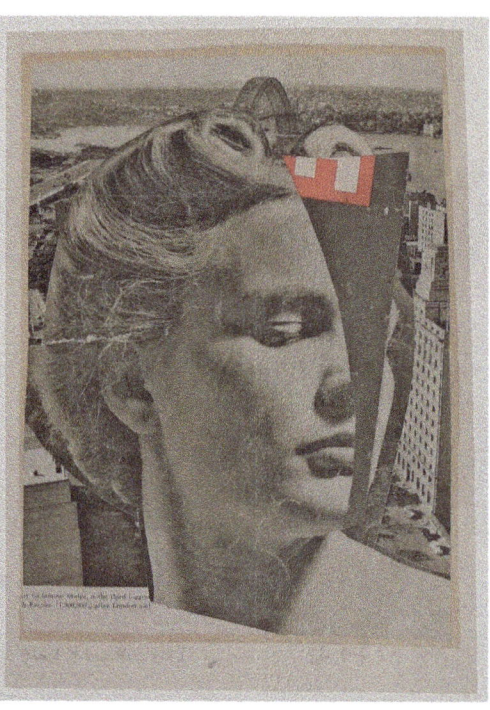

"Right half of a Romantic" Padgett 2022 after
"Left half of a beauty" Schwitters 1947

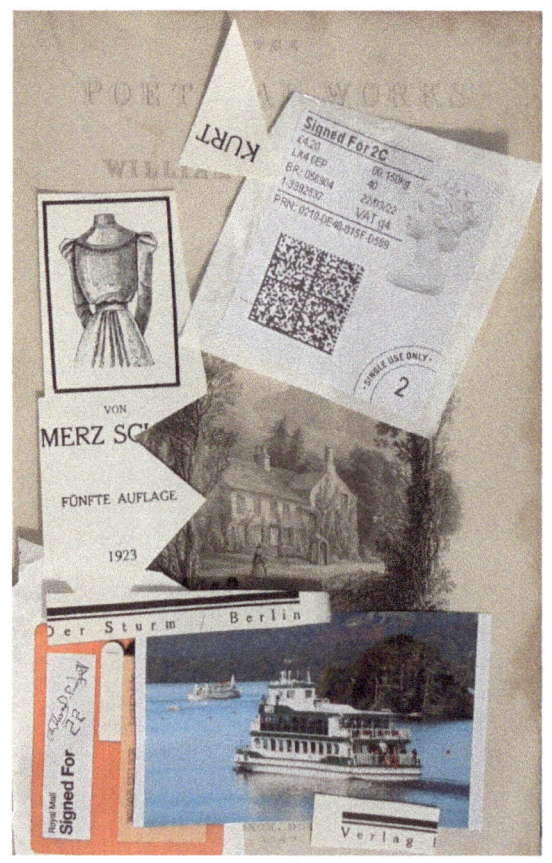

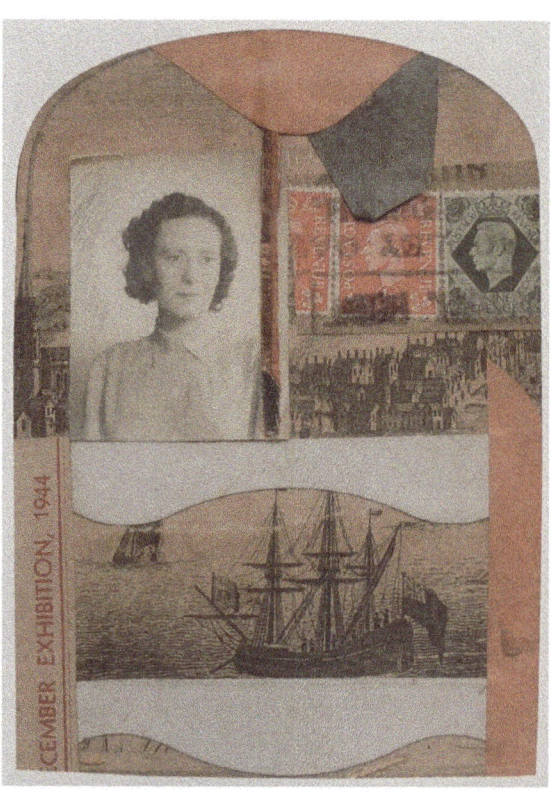

"Rydal Mount Merz" Padgett 2022 after
"mz22 Wantee" Schwitters 1947

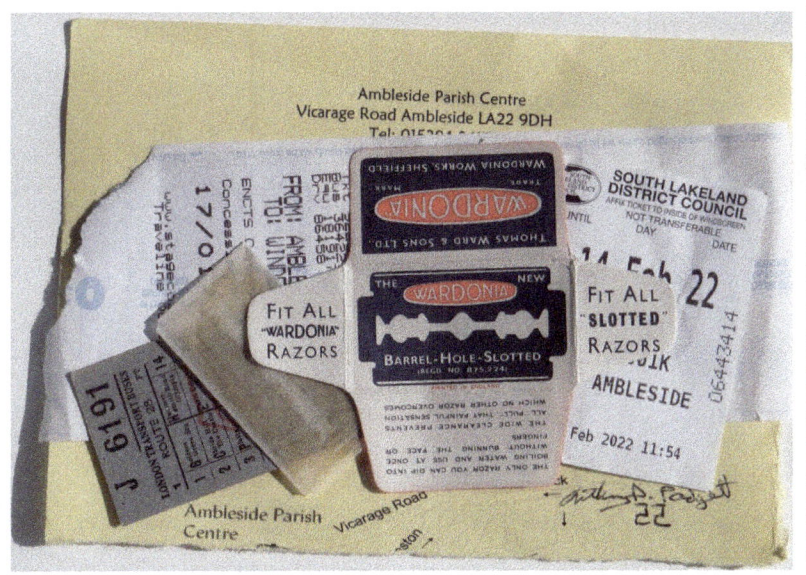

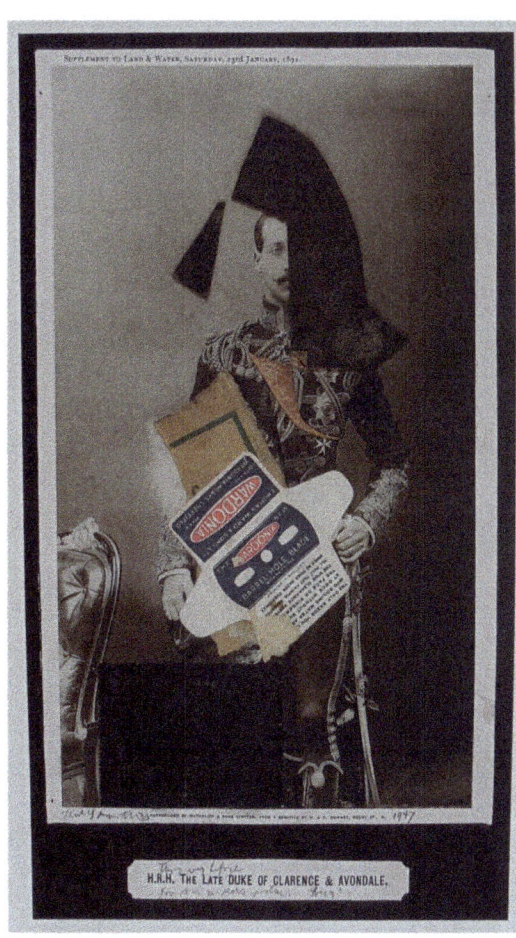

"Ambleside visit" Padgett 2021 after "Duke of Clarence" Schwitters 1947

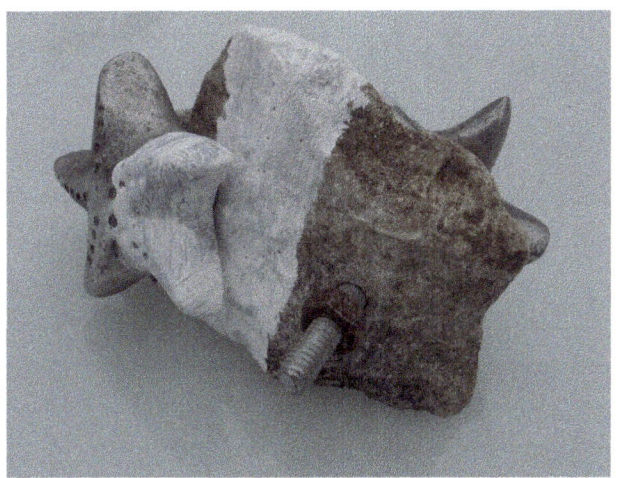

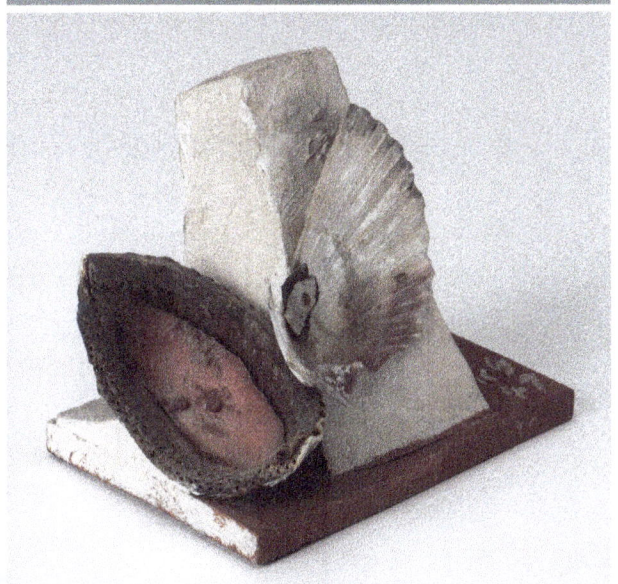

"Starfish" Padgett 2022 after "Shell" Schwitters 1947

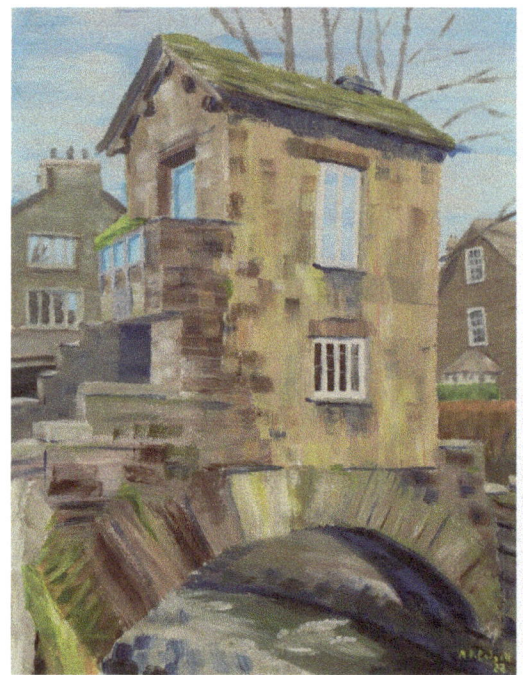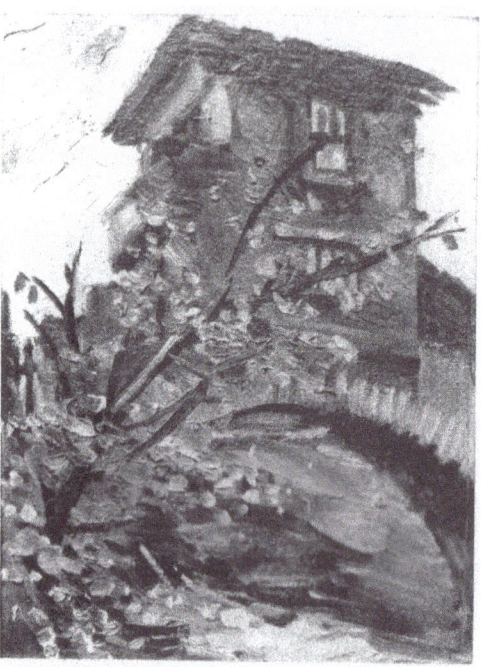

"Bridge House" Padgett 2022 after "Bridge House Ambleside" Schwitters c.1945

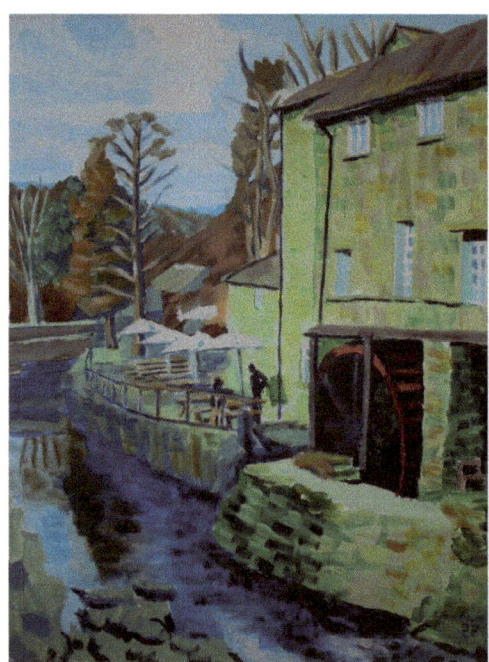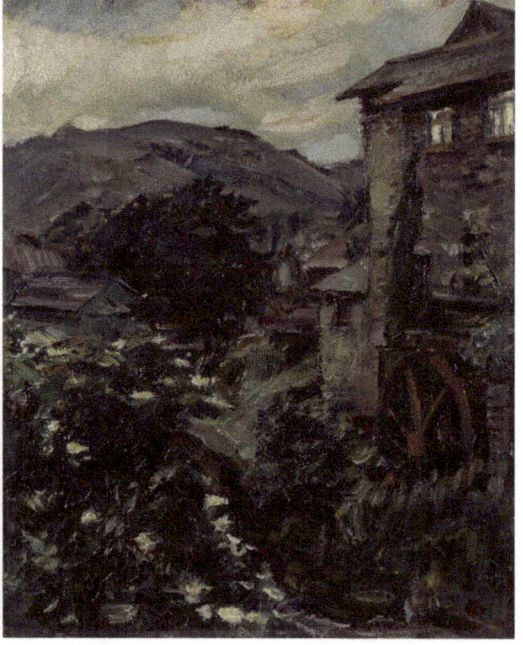

"Old Mill Ambleside" Padgett 2022 after " " Schwitters 1919

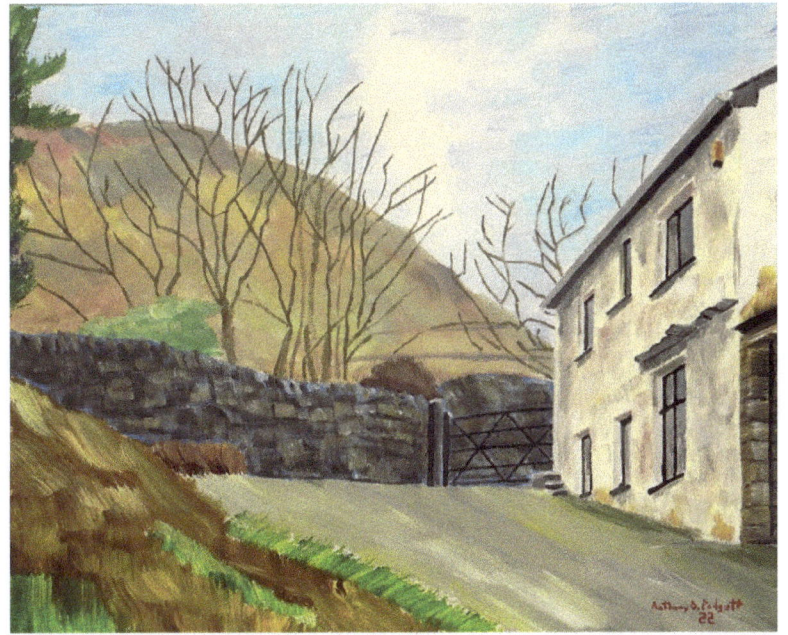

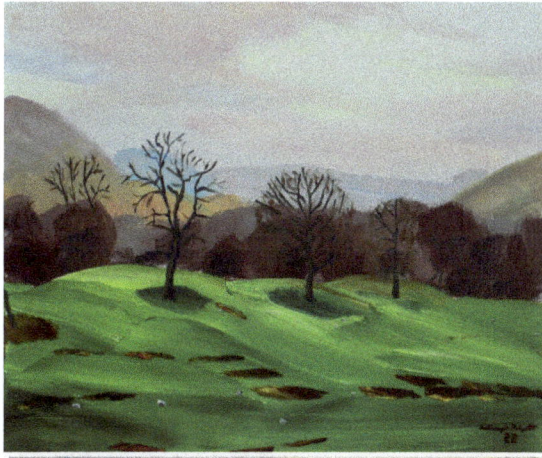

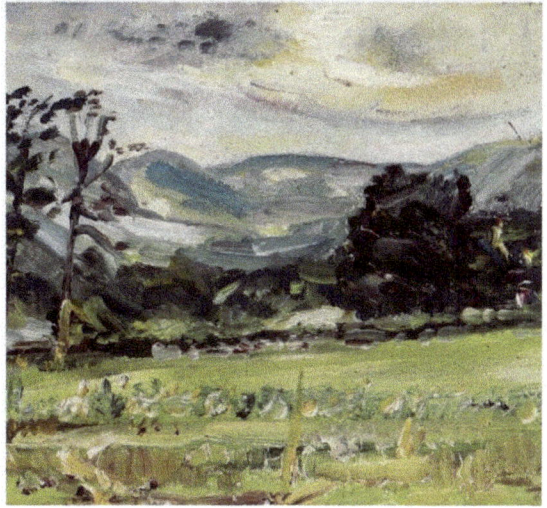

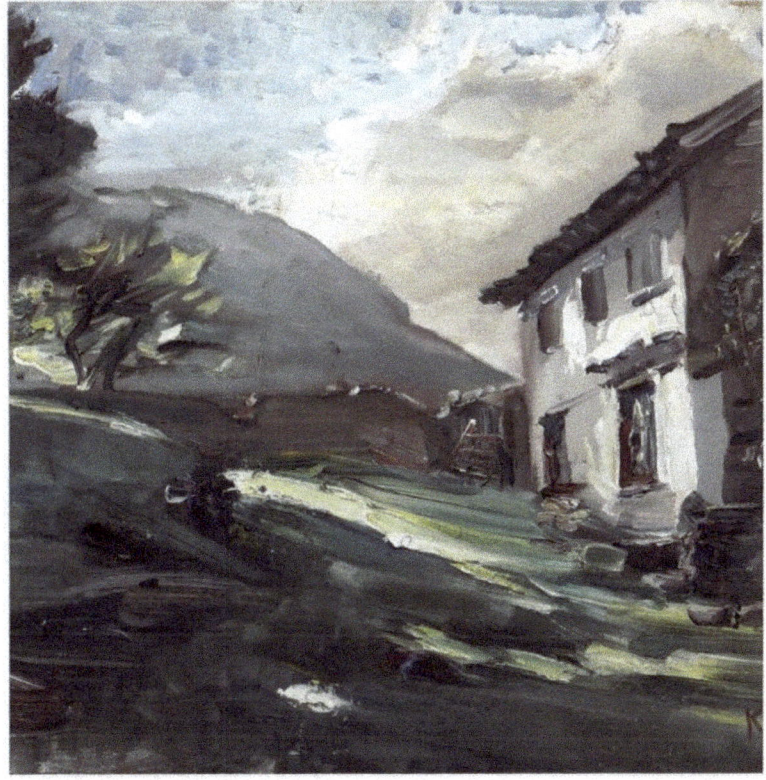

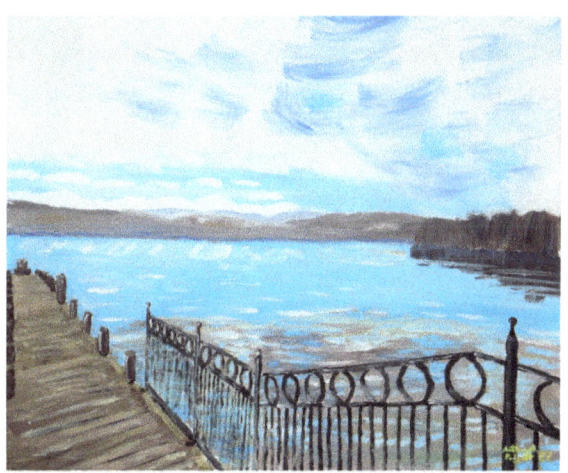

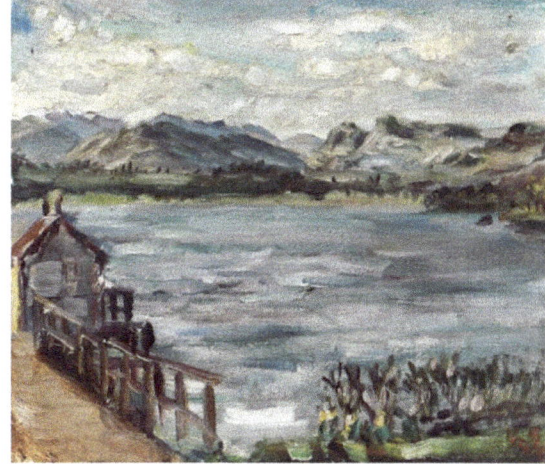

"Helm Crag" Padgett 2022
after Schwitters c.1946

"Under Loughrigg" Padgett 2022
afer Schwitters c.1946

"View from Low Wood" Padgett 2022
after Schwitters c.1946

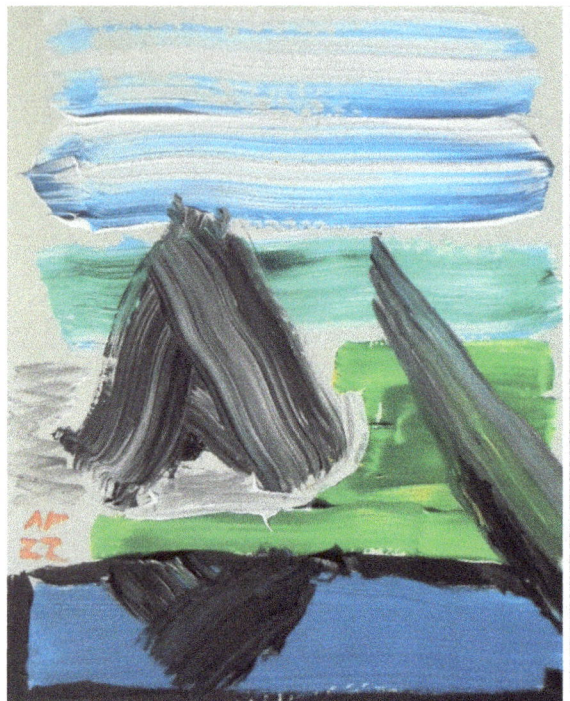
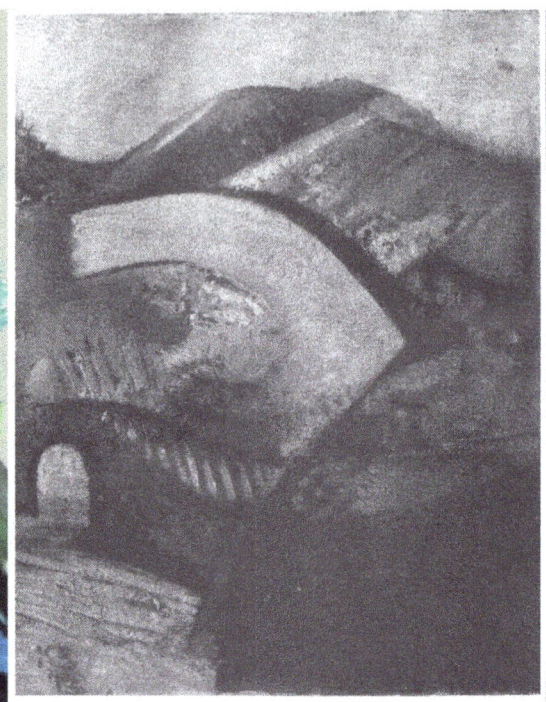

"Grasmere" Padgett 2022
after "Landscape of Grasmere" Schwitters 1942

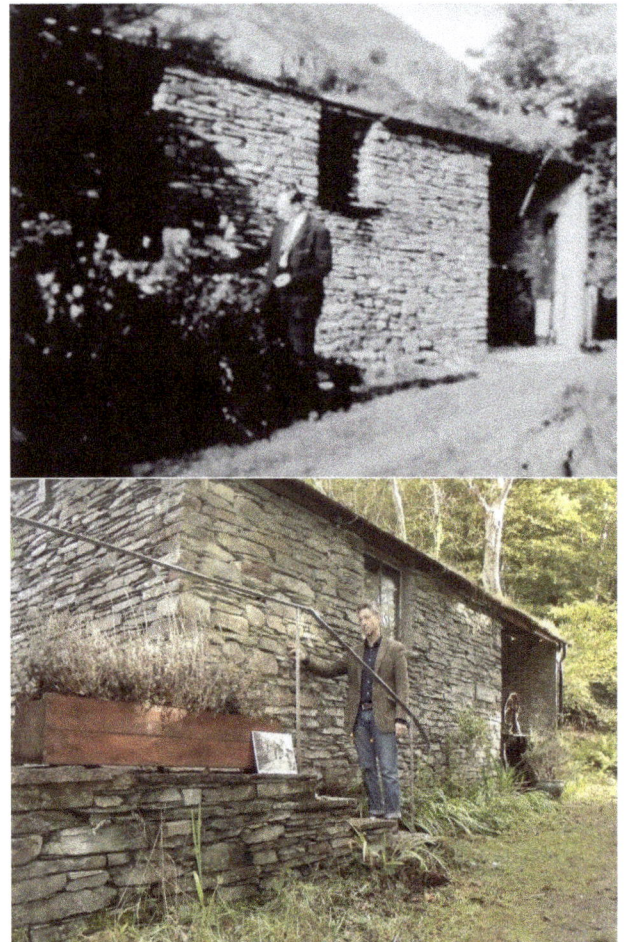

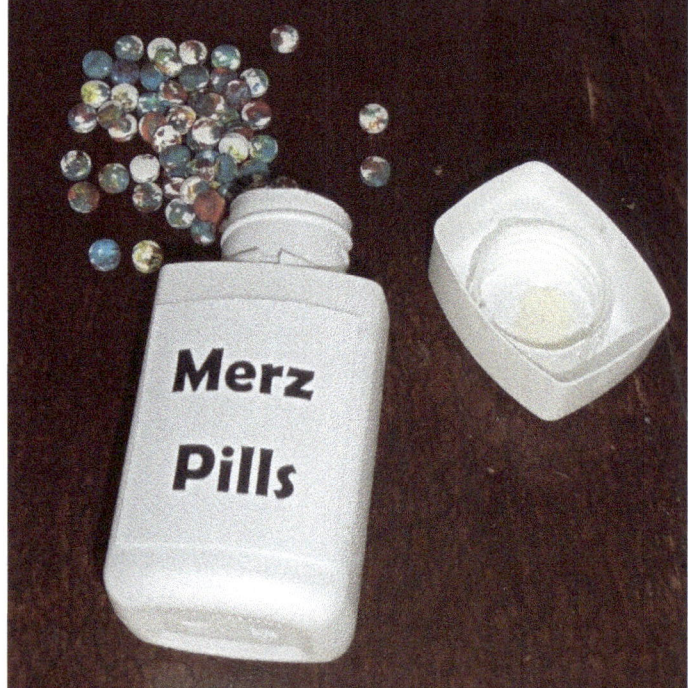

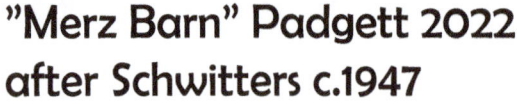

"Merz Barn" Padgett 2022
after Schwitters c.1947

"Merz Pill" Padgett 2022 after
"Merz barn" Schwitters 1947

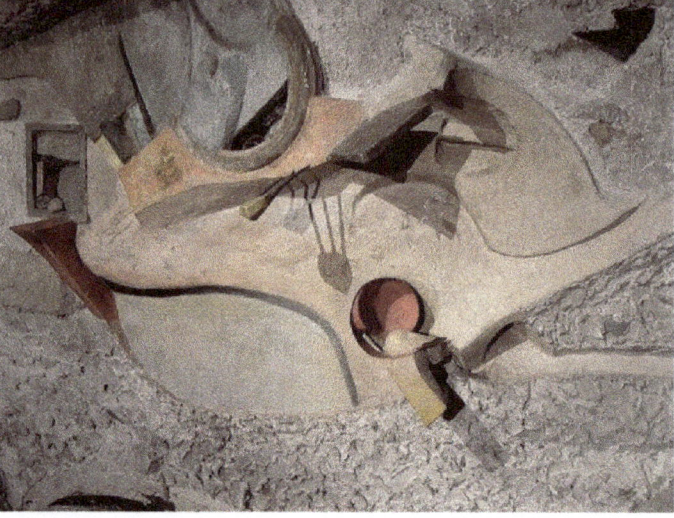

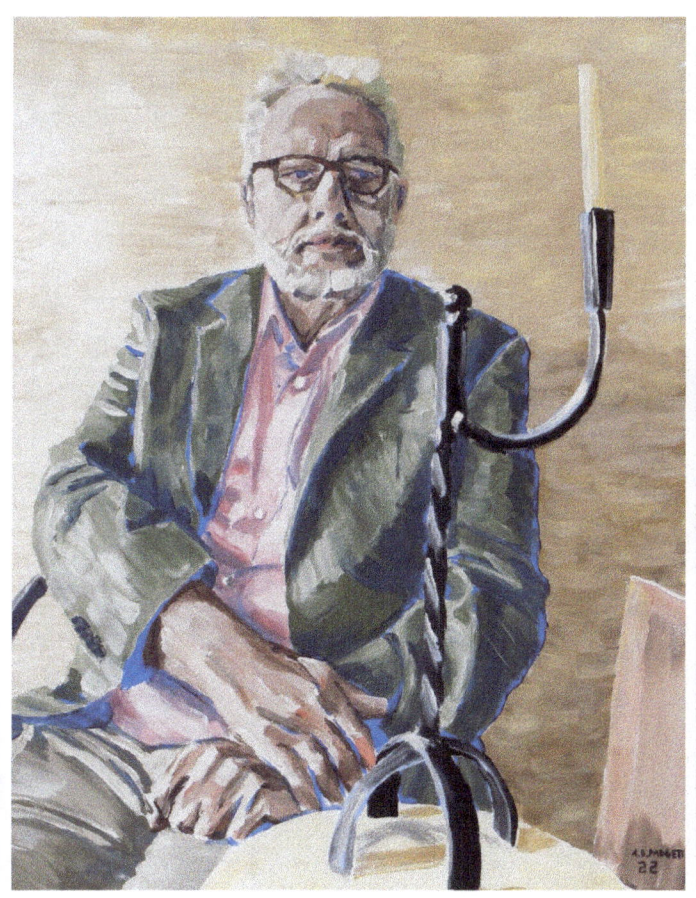
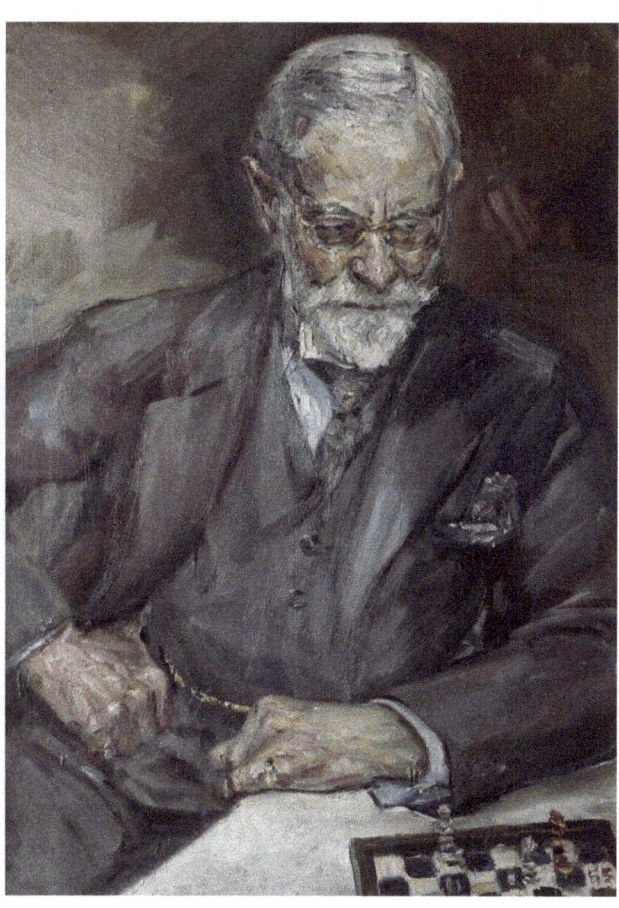

"Dr Sydney Chapman " Padgett 2022
after "Dr Johnston" Schwitters 1946

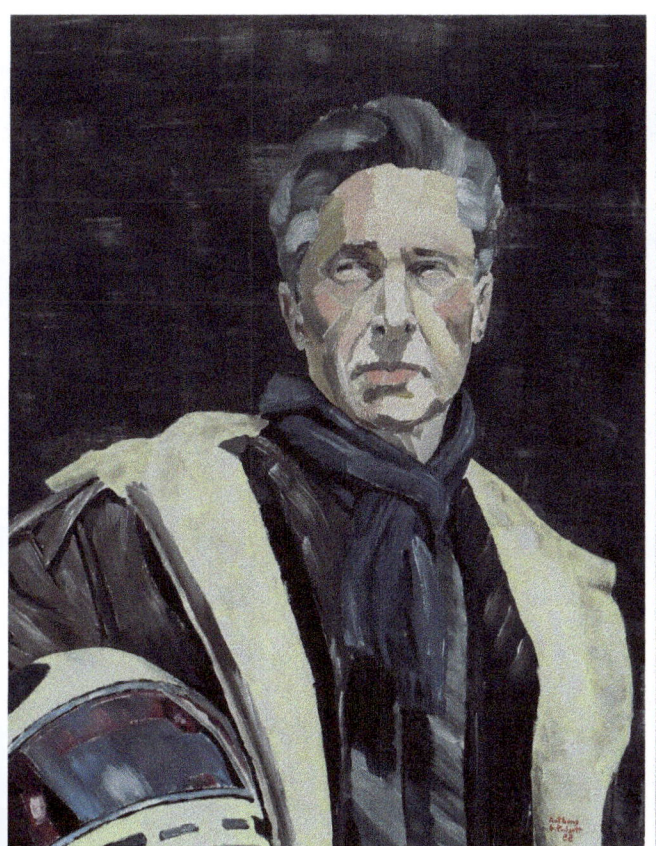
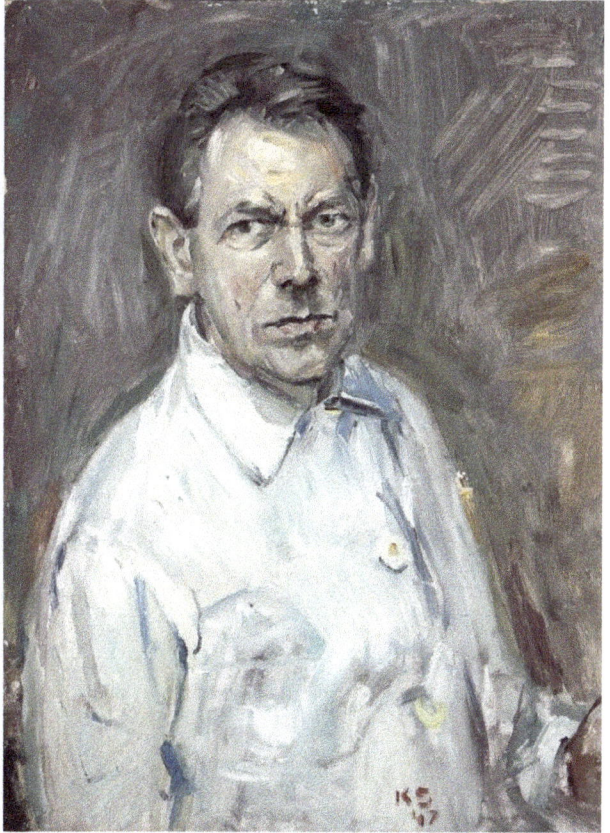

"Self-portrait" Padgett 2022
after "Self-portrait" Schwitters 1947

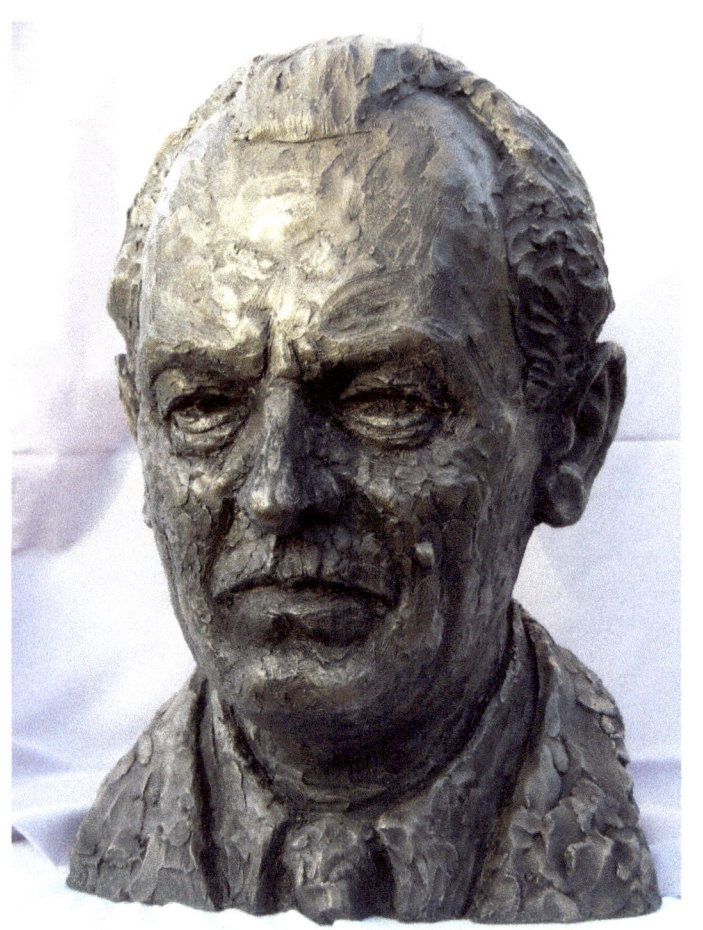

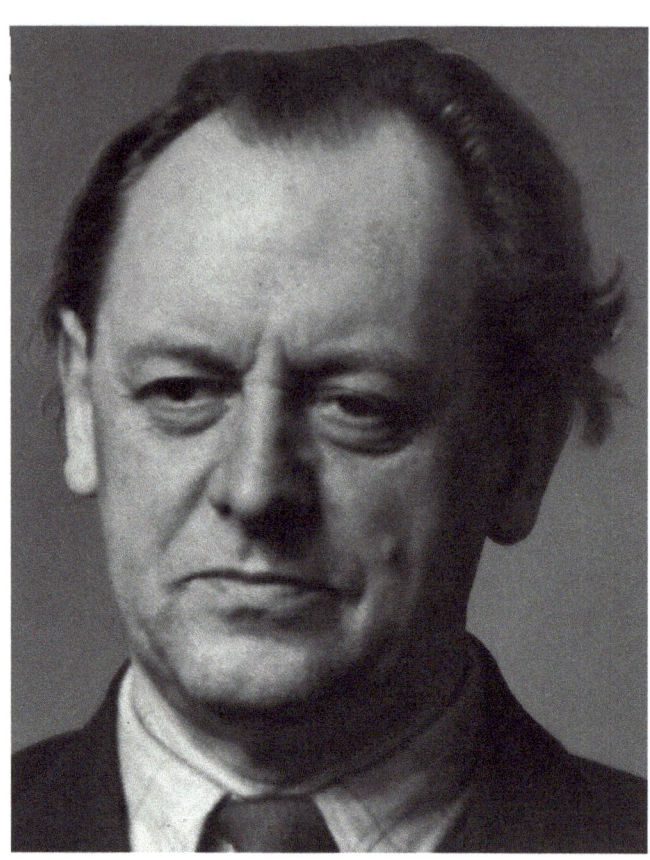

"Bust of Schwitters" Padgett 2022

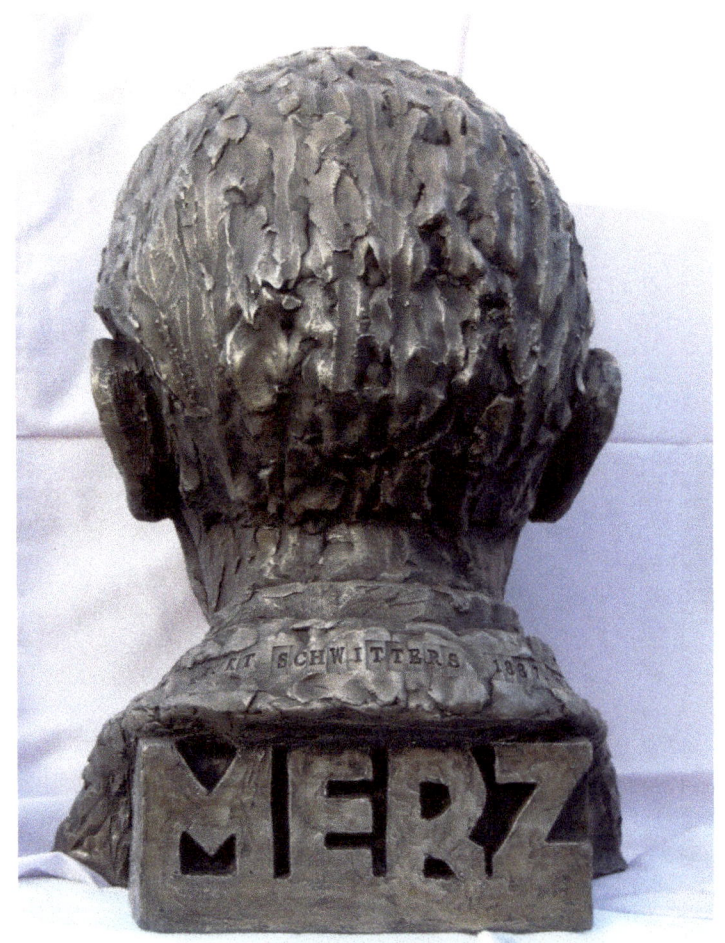

"Bust of Schwitters
(rear)" Padgett 2022

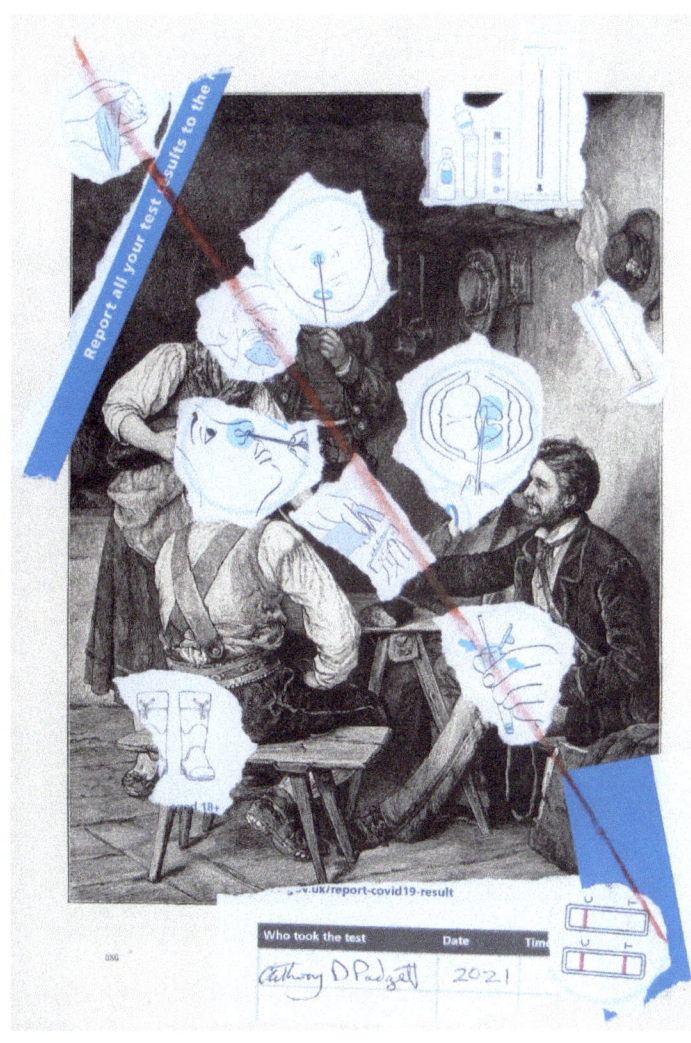

"Who took the test?" Padgett 2021

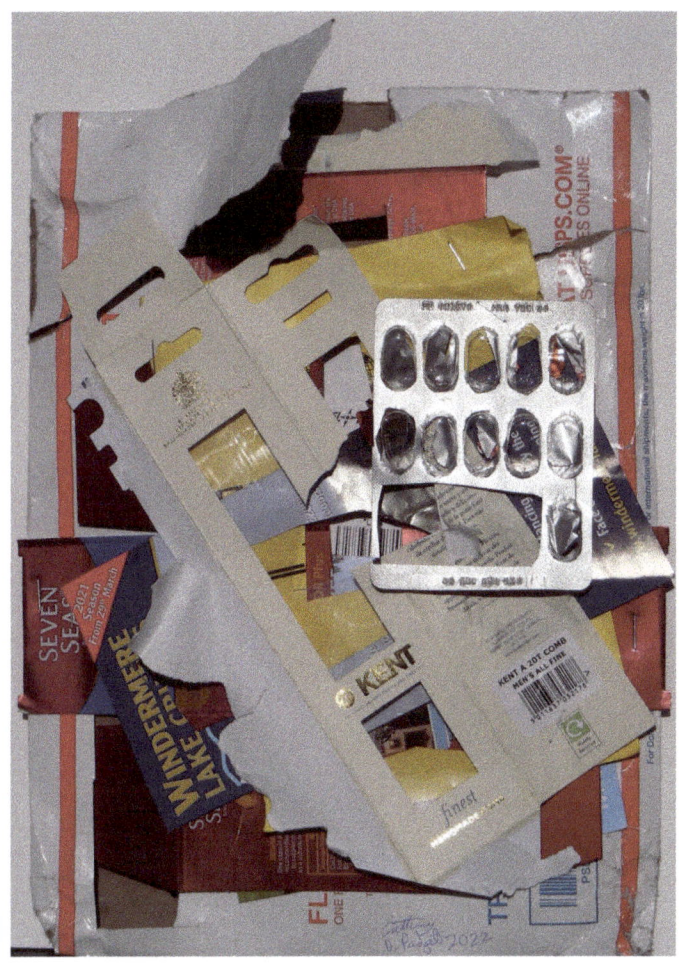

"Ambleside Grave of Schwitters"
Padgett 2022

"Leftover Frames" Padgett
2022

"Merzball" Padgett 2021

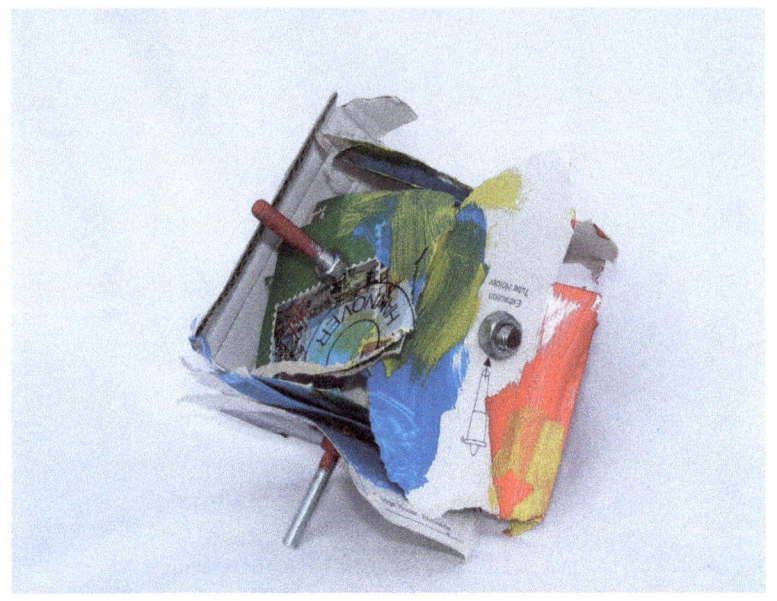

"Lakeland Pencils"
Padgett 2021

"Morecambe Board"
Padgett 2022

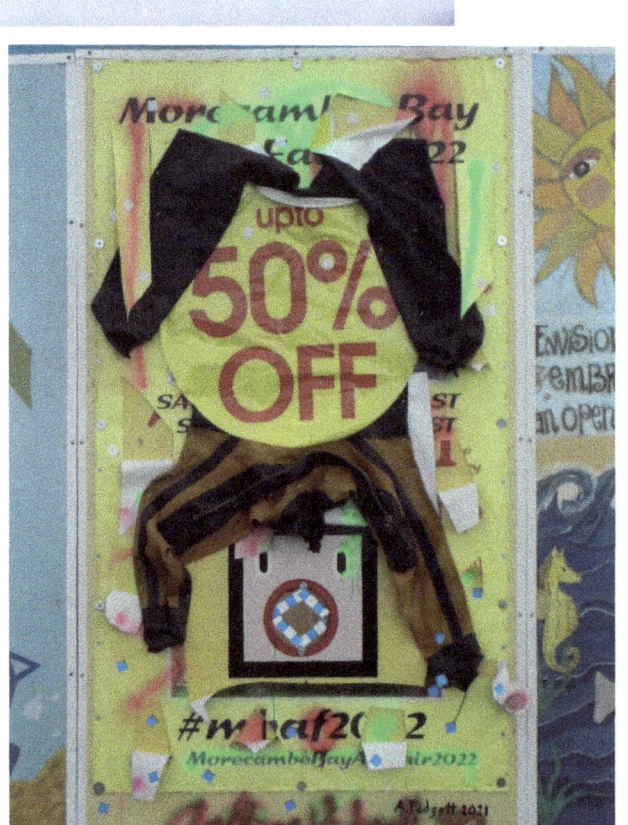

"A Year With Kurt Schwitters"
by Anthony D Padgett
ART DISPLAY
Wednesday 1st - 29th June 2022
Ambleside Library
Kelsick Road, Ambleside, Cumbria, LA22 0BZ

Revisiting scenes and people Schwitters painted whilst living in Ambleside.
OPEN:
Monday 9:30am–1pm
Wednesday 9:30am–1pm, 2–5pm
Friday 9:30am–1pm

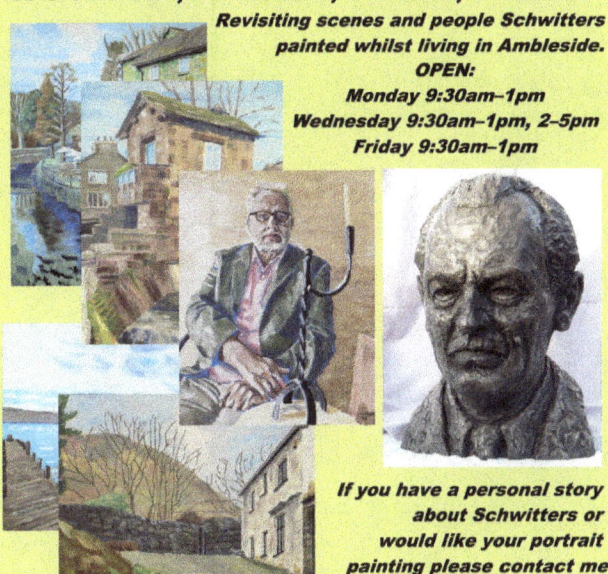

If you have a personal story about Schwitters or would like your portrait painting please contact me anthonydpadgett@yahoo.co.uk

INSTAGRAM: artistdancerwriter - 0790 2342448
Facebook: A Year With Kurt Schwitters

"A Year With Kurt Schwitters"
by Anthony D Padgett
ART Exhibition
7th September - 1st October 2022
Kendal Library
Stricklandgate, Kendal, Cumbria, LA9 4PY

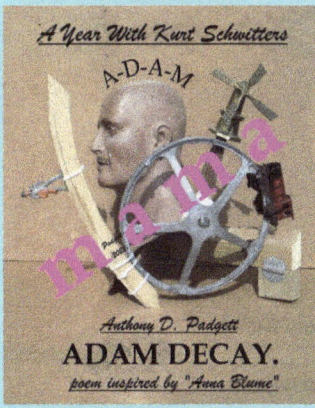
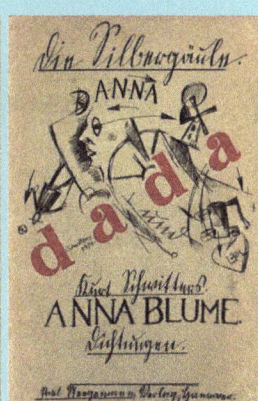

Artist's Talk: The Romantic Art & Poetry of Kurt Schwitters
Thursday 22nd September 3-4.30pm

Padgett's painting, collage, sculpture & poetry in response to the work of Kurt Schwitters. And his collection of rare Schwitters books

INSTAGRAM: artistdancerwriter   Mob:0790 2342448
EMAIL: anthonydpadgett@yahoo.co.uk
Facebook: A Year With Kurt Schwitters

Saturday 15th October 2022
7.30pm - 11.30pm   *1920s & 1940s Vintage Style*

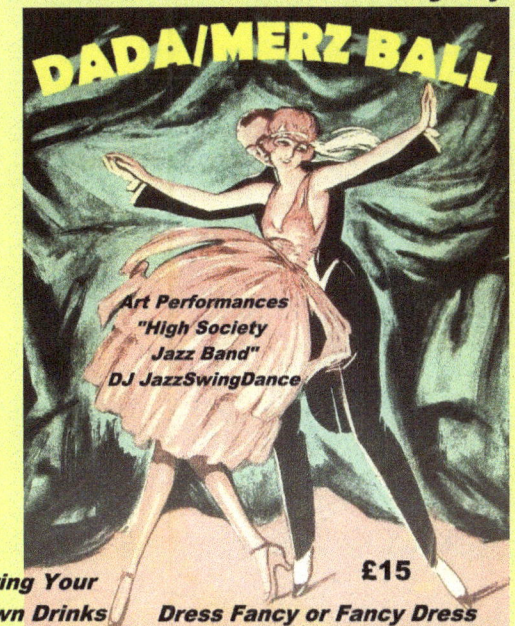

DADA/MERZ BALL

Art Performances
"High Society Jazz Band"
DJ JazzSwingDance

Bring Your Own Drinks   **£15**
Dress Fancy or Fancy Dress
Prize for best decorated table
St Mary's Civic Hall, The Centre,
Vicarage Rd, Ambleside LA22 9DH
anthonydpadgett@yahoo.co.uk Mob: 07902342448
INSTAGRAM: ArtistDancerWriter
Facebook: A Year With Kurt Schwitters

Saturday 15th October 2022
1st Annual Ambleside DADA/MERZ BALL !
**St Mary's Civic Hall,
Vicarage Rd,
Ambleside LA22 9DH**

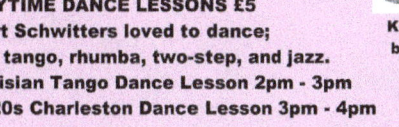

Kurt Schwitters
by A.D.Padgett

DAYTIME DANCE LESSONS £5
Kurt Schwitters loved to dance;
the tango, rhumba, two-step, and jazz.
Parisian Tango Dance Lesson 2pm - 3pm
1920s Charleston Dance Lesson 3pm - 4pm

DADA/MERZ BALL
7.30pm - 11.30pm
Performances 8pm
Live Music and
Dancing from 9pm
Table Award 10pm

High Society Jazz Band

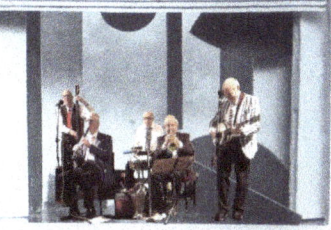

*Bring Your
Own Drinks*

*1920s & 1940s
Vintage Style*   **Dress Fancy or Fancy Dress**

OPEN MIC: Email me to do an Art Performance
anthonydpadgett@yahoo.co.uk
Mobile: 0790 2342448
£15   **INSTAGRAM ArtistDancerWriter**
Facebook: A Year With Kurt Schwitters

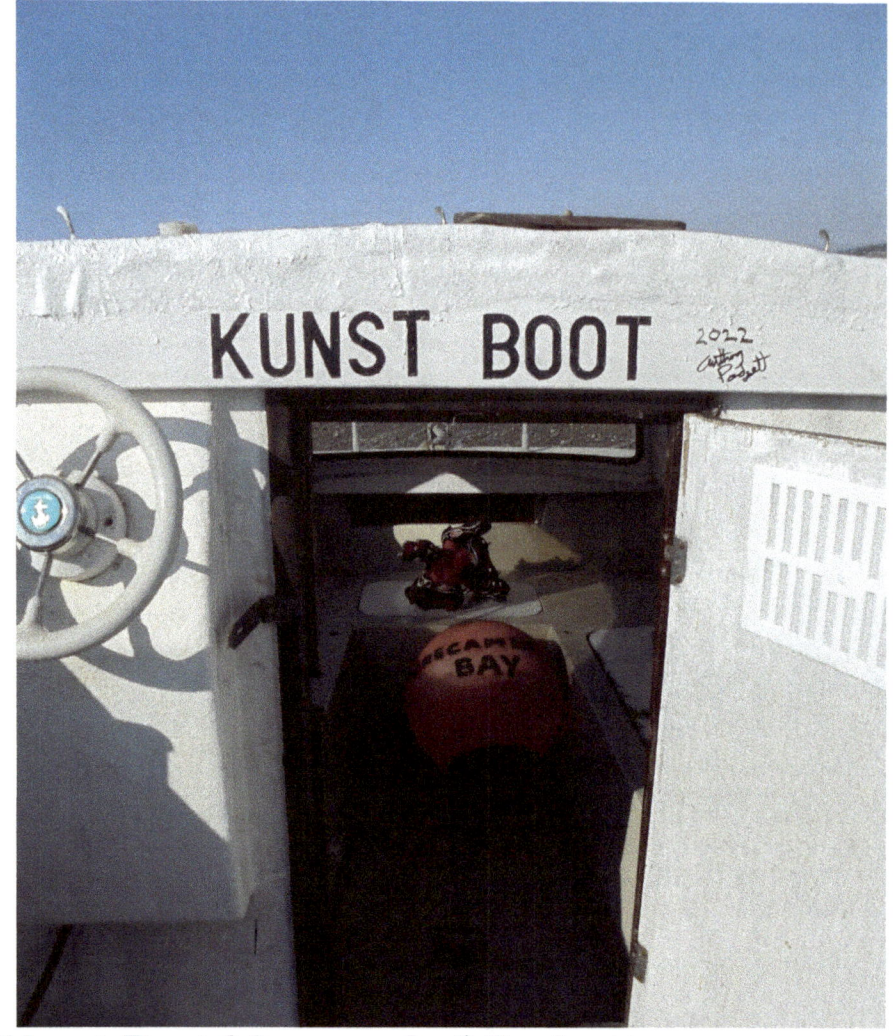

"Kunst Boot Morecambe" Padgett 2022

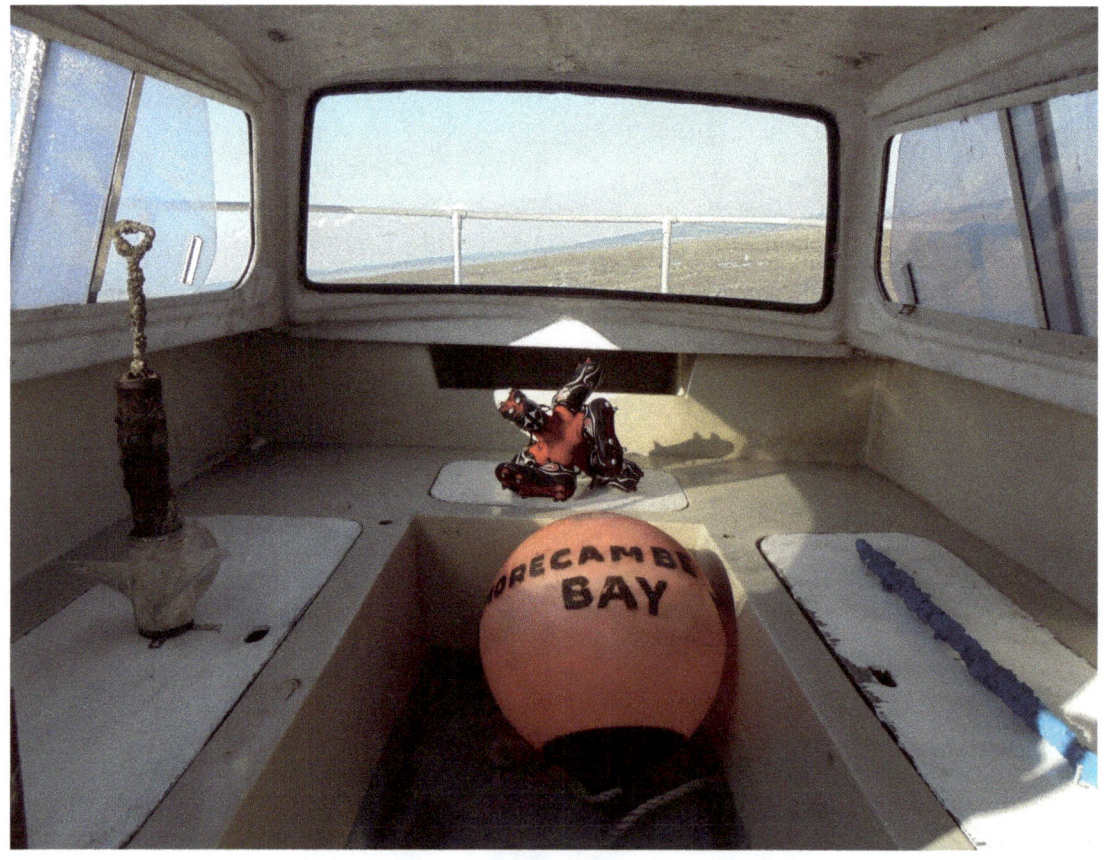

"Merz Exhibition" Padgett 2022

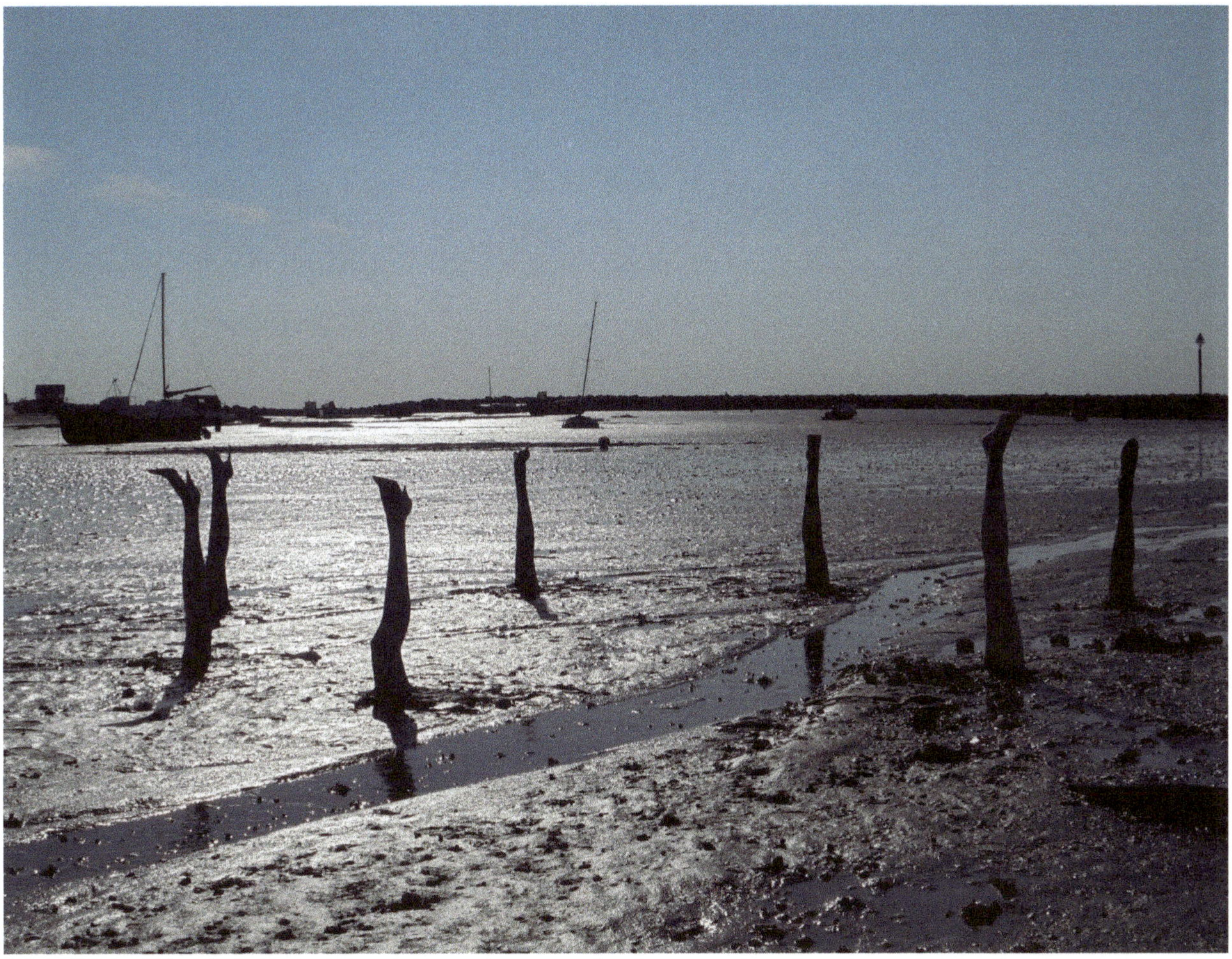

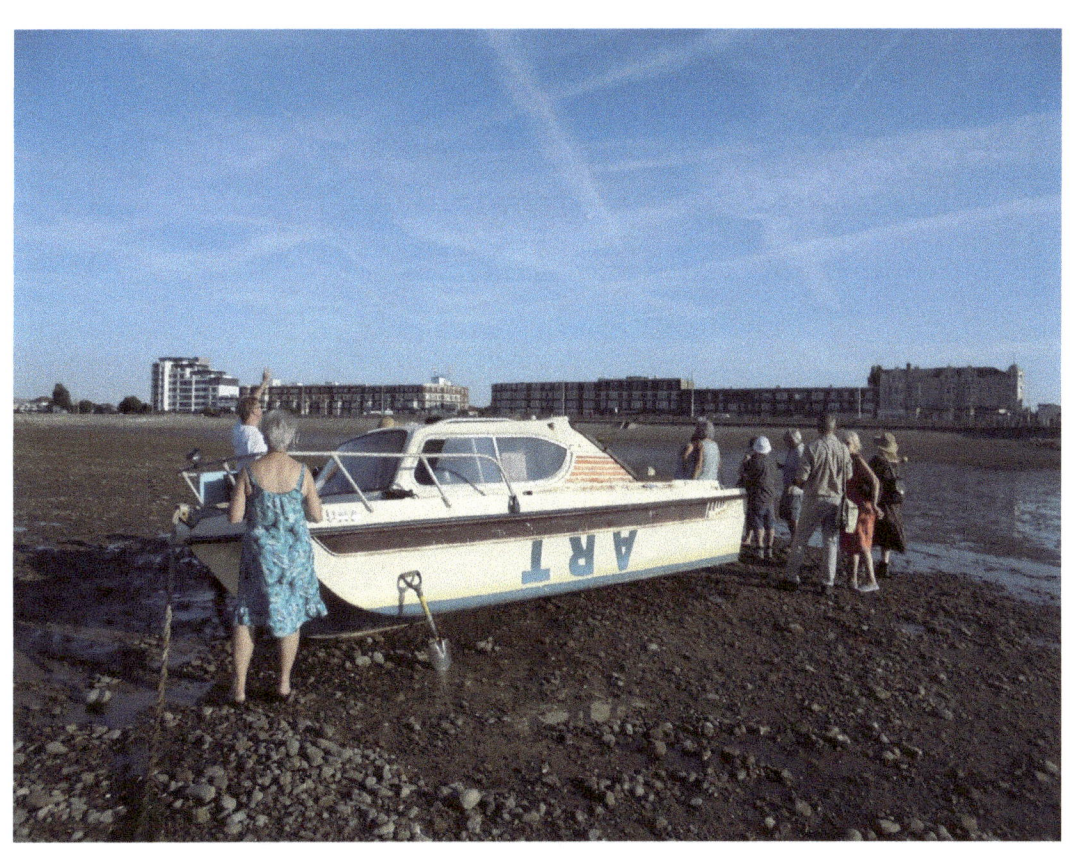

"Sea Legs" Padgett 2022

"Merz Exhibition" Padgett 2022

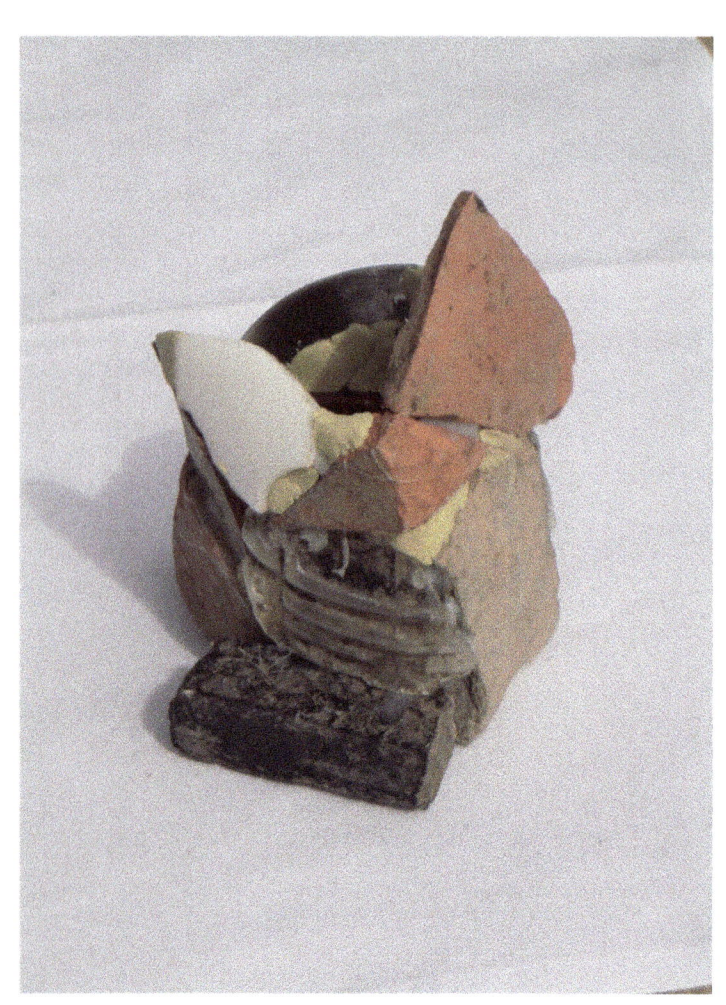

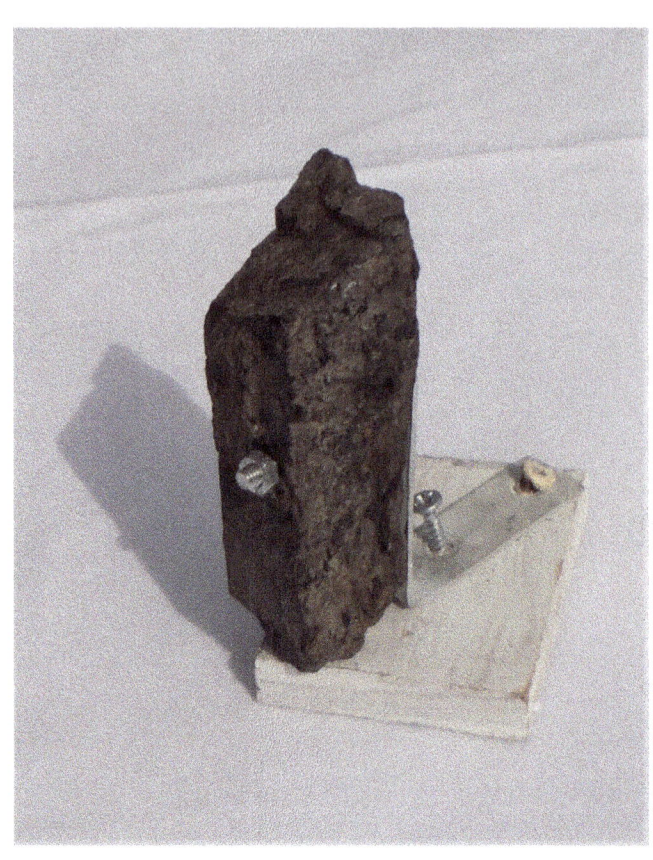

"Armitt Cup", "Armitt Coal"
and "Armitt Coal Cup"
Padgett 2022

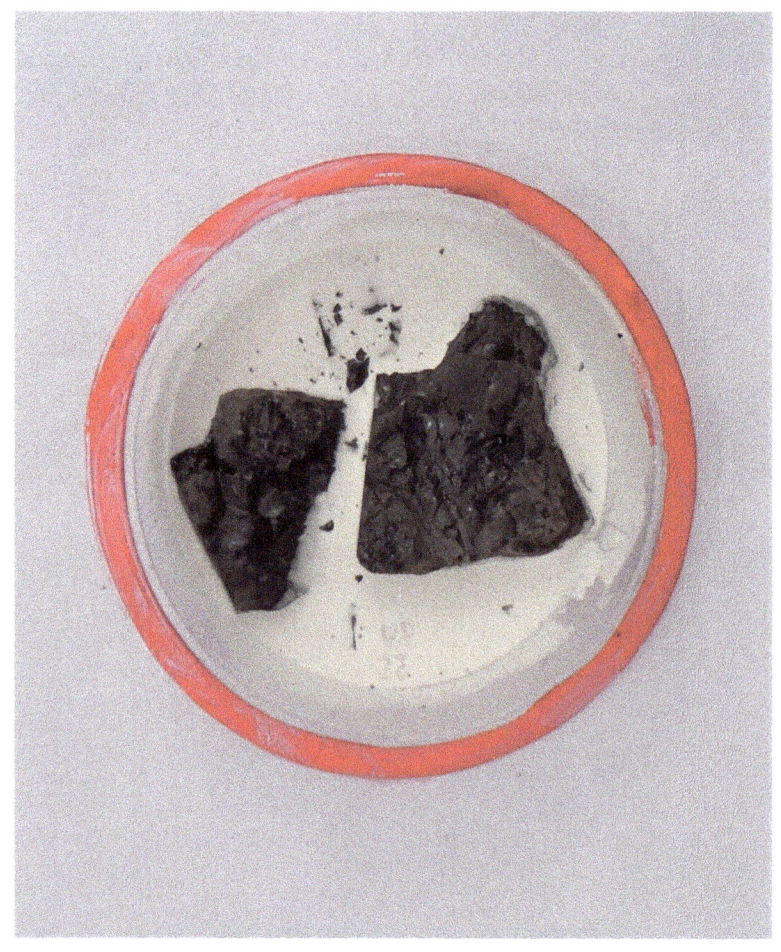

fin........

www.ingramcontent.com/pod-product-compliance
Lightning Source LLC
Chambersburg PA
CBHW050145180526
45172CB00011B/1321